Love and Quasars

Love and Quasars

An Astrophysicist Reconciles Faith and Science

Paul Wallace

FORTRESS PRESS
MINNEAPOLIS

LOVE AND QUASARS
An Astrophysicist Reconciles Faith and Science

Cover image: iStock 847261704 by Adventure_Photo

Cover design: Lindsey Owens

Print ISBN: 978-1-5064-4843-5

eBook ISBN: 978-1-5064-4844-2

The paper used in this publication meets the minimum requirements of American National Standard for Information Sciences — Permanence of Paper for Printed Library Materials, ANSI Z329.48-1984.

Manufactured in the U.S.A.

For Scary Mom

Contents

Introduction: What This Book Is about and How It Works

Years ago, on a clear October evening, I saw Uranus with my naked eye. My lab assistant and I stayed behind at the college observatory after all the Astronomy 101 students had departed for the night, and we devoted ourselves to the project. It took some effort, but we both succeeded in spotting the seventh planet amid the stars scattered along the Aquarius-Pisces boundary, with no help from binoculars or telescopes.

Uranus sits just this side of visibility and moves slowly, taking eighty-four years to complete a single lap around the sun. For these reasons, it spent many years cataloged as a star. Then, in 1781, an Englishman named William Herschel observed it through his homemade telescope, thought it looked odd, and recorded it as a comet. Within a couple of years, however, astronomers overruled this assignment and announced the first discovery of a planet in recorded history.

Herschel named it George. Non-British astronomers, uninterested in honoring King George III of England, weren't having it. Scientists haggled over the name for decades, and the planet was finally given its permanent moniker in 1850. Uranus jokes began appearing in print shortly thereafter.[1]

In order to see Uranus with your naked eye, you must meet certain requirements. First, you need to be under a truly dark sky. Humidity, city lights, moonlight, or any combination of these brighten the sky so much that Uranus will be wiped clean out. You must also have excellent vision, a star chart showing the exact location of Uranus among the stars at the time of observation, and plenty of patience.

With all this, however, you could still look and look and look and not spot it. In fact, you could stare directly at Uranus for hours without knowing it. The source of this puzzlement dwells not in the heavens but in your eye. The human retina contains two kinds of light-detecting cells, cones and rods. Cones respond to colors and bright lights and are concentrated at the center of the retina, opposite the lens. Rods detect low levels of light and are spread out around the cones. When you look at Uranus straight on, the light falls on the cones, but the planet glows too faintly to be detected by these cells. You'll never see Uranus by looking *at* it.

But if you look just to the side of it, its light falls on your rods, and the planet pops into view. Once this happens, you instinctively move your eye back toward it and, *poof*, it disappears again. Resisting this reflex feels weird at first, but with practice, the technique becomes natural. Experienced stargazers are accustomed to using this so-called *averted vision* to see dim objects.

Much as some things can be seen not by looking at them but by looking at what is next to them, some things can be understood not by thinking about them but by thinking about what is next to them. The more you think about these things or try to figure them out or nail them down, the more elusive they become. They can't be grasped by head-on thinking. But if you relax a little and think to the side, you might come to know what you could never comprehend directly.

Take God, for example. We all want to know and understand God, but the Lord is tough to get a fix on. Just ask

Moses. He was pretty tight with Yahweh, but despite asking for more, and asking nicely, he never got to see more than God's backside. Mostly God appeared to Moses as something else: a burning bush, a pillar of fire, a cloud. Isaiah saw the lining of God's robes, not God. Jacob wrestled with God in the form of a man he couldn't see, and angels often stand in the gap between God and human beings.

In addition to offering us such stories, Scripture tells us plainly that God abides beyond understanding and creates beyond imagination: "For my thoughts are not your thoughts, nor are your ways my ways, says the Lord. For as the heavens are higher than the earth, so are my ways higher than your ways and my thoughts than your thoughts" (Isaiah 55:8–9). Given all this, our gaining insight into God appears as unlikely as a panda gaining insight into particle physics. The gap between us and the Creator seems impossibly wide.

But God desires to be present with us. Jesus, of course, manifests that desire. But I'm convinced that we may also find the Creator in the world around us. Like averting one's vision in order to see Uranus, we can glimpse God by relaxing our eyes a little and looking at what's *next* to God—a friend, a community, a bird, a landscape, a cosmos.

But it's not so easy, is it? Over the centuries, we've looked closer and closer at the universe and its contents, and many people haven't glimpsed God in it, or next to it, or anywhere else for that matter. In fact, scientists—the very ones who have done the most careful and systematic looking at what I claim is next to God—are relatively unlikely to believe in God at all. Some prominent scientists have even made careers out of speaking and writing *against* God. They believe science demonstrates that, like the emperor in the folk tale, faith spends its days marching around the town square with no clothes on.

Some believers seem to agree. They, too, think science removes God from the world, so they work hard to discredit science. Many Christians have singled out the big bang and evolution as particular threats to true faith. Also, plenty of nonscientists and nonbelievers look at the news, see headlines about the conflict between faith and science, and assume the two naturally oppose one another or, at best, have nothing helpful to say to each other.

So if we can see God by looking at the world, why is it so many people don't?

I can think of two reasons. First, many people hold an unrealistic view of science, believing it provides an unbiased and comprehensive view of reality. Beyond this, certain public voices claim not only that science reveals the truth but also that it alone has the capacity to do so.

This is false. When we view the cosmos through the lenses of science, we see an incomplete picture, because those lenses filter out certain aspects of the world the way sunglasses filter out certain wavelengths of light. For example, virtues such as faith, hope, and love—as well as their shadow sides of distrust, despair, and fear—are blocked by the shades of science. About these values, science has nothing to report. In the eyes of science, in fact, they don't even exist.

But if the lenses of science work like sunglasses, they work like *prescription* sunglasses: they sharpen and refine what we *can* see through them. We don't need science to know about faith, hope, and love, but we'd never be aware of such realities as evolution, atoms, and quasars without it.

The second reason people don't see God in the world is that, as science has expanded, faith has remained small. It hasn't evolved. More often than not, it has retreated from the world and closed off the possibility of finding God anywhere outside the box of belief and belonging called *church*. What we see through scientific glasses may be incomplete, but it's also real, and faith must account for it. But faith has become narrow and rigid and either aligned itself against the cosmos (a losing proposition if ever there was one) or ignored it altogether. In both cases, it has failed to engage science meaningfully and remains incapable of dealing honestly and openly with the cosmos that science has revealed.

This failure has consequences. Several years ago, a major survey sought to pinpoint why young people are leaving the church. One of the principal reasons had to do with science; the survey found that a large percentage of young adults agree with the statements "Churches come across as antagonistic toward science," "Churches are out of step with the scientific world we live in," "Christianity is anti-science," and "[I am] turned off by the creation-versus-evolution debate."[2]

In *Love and Quasars* I address this problem in two ways. First, I demonstrate the ways in which science is limited. Second, I outline some features of a faith large enough to encompass both love *and* the cosmos—a faith that might know and love God by knowing and loving what is next to God.

This is a large task for a little book, so here's a brief road map to help you navigate *Love and Quasars*. The first two chapters describe the faith-and-science problem, the following two lay out four popular solutions, and the fifth chapter offers my reconciliation of faith and science. The remaining chapters apply my solution to a range of topics, including God, Scripture, the problem of death and suffering, miracles, history, atheism, and the meaning of faith itself.

A few clarifications before we lift off: By *faith*, I mean

not only the religion of Christianity past and present but also our communal and individual experiences and beliefs and practices associated with that religion. By *cosmos* or *universe*, I mean the entirety of physical and biological reality, not just the outer-space part of it. And by *science*, unless otherwise indicated, I mean the systematic exploration of the cosmos and the creation of theories through observations and controlled experiments, not technological spin-offs and advances made possible by this exploration and theory building.

Love and Quasars has been made possible by my family, friends, Agnes Scott College, and all the good earthlings at Fortress Press, the John Templeton Foundation, and the Science for Youth Ministry Project at Luther Seminary. I am particularly grateful to my editor, Tony Jones, who has in the course of this project demonstrated exactitude and patience in equal measure. Finally, as he has done before, my brother Keith Pierce read through the manuscript and offered his valuable insight, and I thank him for it.

Now let's get this thing off the ground.

1.

Two Ways of Seeing the Sun: Through the Eyes of Faith or the Eyes of Science?

My family and I were heading west across the rice fields of Arkansas when I pointed out the window and said five words I would come to regret. We were bound for the annual Wallace family reunion in London (population 699) on the far side of the state. The drive from Atlanta and back was an annual rite during my formative years; we completed the trip every Thanksgiving from my early childhood until the fall after I graduated from college. Once we arrived in London, the grown-ups would sit around and yak while we kids would meet up with the cousins, play football, shoot up aluminum cans, set off fireworks over the lake, and walk the railroad tracks. Old and young alike ate lots of Southern food.

We had crossed the Mississippi River, and the world had flattened out around us. From the back seat, I saw the late-afternoon sun shining through clouds, making rays, bright rays, spreading out across the plain ahead. The beams stood out against dark clouds in the distance. Awed, I pointed over the Catalina's bench seat and said, "That's the glory of God."

My words must have made quite an impression on Dad, because he laughed out loud and, over the following years, told lots of people about what I'd said. He would describe the road trip and the eastern Arkansas plains and the sunbeams. Then he would point as I had pointed, repeat my words, and laugh, looking at me—all pleased and expectant, as if he wanted me to laugh, too.

But I never did. I hated the story, and the older I got, the more I hated it. For decades, I didn't know why he did it—why he picked that story and why he kept reminding me and everyone else of that one thing I said that one day and which we all would have forgotten if he didn't keep bringing it up over and over.

In the early years, I would sometimes stand in the living room outside Dad's home office and listen to him make business calls. A civil engineer specializing in hydrology and nuclear waste, he talked confidently about runoff and the water table and strontium half-lives. I didn't understand what he was talking about, but I loved listening to him anyway. His voice was direct and serious. I wanted to talk like that, too, but "That's the glory of God" was not, to my mind, serious. These were little-kid words, and they embarrassed me. They made me seem simple and sentimental, and I didn't want to be thought of that way, especially by Dad. Whenever he'd tell the story and laugh, I felt as if he was laughing at *me*.

I now know that I had no reason to be embarrassed, and on two levels. First, I think I finally understand why Dad loved that story and told it to everyone, and I'm sure that if he had known how much I hated it, he'd have stopped immediately and forever. Second, my response to the sunset was immediate and true in the way of children and saints. If I'd been older that day in Arkansas, I might have spoken these words from Saint Francis:

Be Praised, Lord, through all your creatures,
especially through my lord Brother Sun,
who brings the day; and You give light through him.
And he is beautiful and radiant in all his splendor!
Of You, Most High, he bears the likeness.[1]

But I was eight years old, so I said, "That's the glory of God" and set myself up for years of embarrassment.

Later, in college, I learned some science, and it was official science, too: physics, very grown-up, very unsentimental. I learned about galaxies and atoms and fundamental forces and space-time. I learned mechanics, electrodynamics, optics, thermodynamics, statistical mechanics, astrophysics, quantum theory, relativity, and atomic and nuclear physics. Also lots of math.

After four years of this, I acquired a new way of seeing that childhood roadside splendor. The sun was no longer the glory of God; it was a gigantic fusion machine. I learned that gravity drives—and contains—an immense and perpetual nuclear explosion in the sun's core. I learned that the light leaving the solar surface (not an actual solid surface, but a layer of plasma called the *photosphere*) starts off as gamma rays in the sun's center, where the temperature exceeds ten million degrees Celsius. I learned that this light requires hundreds of thousands of years to work its way out to the photosphere from the core, but only eight minutes twenty seconds to travel from there to Earth. I learned that the sun had been formed from a vast cloud of gas and dust about four-and-a-half billion years ago, that it had been burning its hydrogen fuel ever since, and that a couple billion more years will pass before its tank goes dry forever. I also learned that sunbeams are called *crepuscular rays*, a fact that brought me a small and special happiness.

A Lecture on the Lake

Early one evening several weeks after I had graduated from college, my family and I were boating on Lake Burton in northeast Georgia, surrounded by the Blue Ridge Mountains. The midsummer haze allowed us to look directly at the sun, again low in the west, without frying our eyes. It sat on the ridge like a five ball on a dinosaur's back, orange and plain. Mom commented on the beauty of the thing. "Gód's handiwork," she called it.

"The sun's not really right there," I said. "It's dropped behind the ridge already. If you drew a line straight toward that orange disc, it would miss the actual sun completely. It would go way over it." I explained how sunlight refracts when it passes from the vacuum of outer space into Earth's atmosphere, how it curves gently down toward the surface of the planet, making the sun appear to be in a location it's not.

"Oh, goodness, Paul, can't you just *enjoy* it?" she asked, smiling but mildly provoked by my turning a fabulous evening on the lake into an optics lecture. Dad smiled to himself as he piloted the boat. I went on about why the sun looks like it's there when it's not really, why it looks orange when it's not really, why it looks kind of flattened out when it's not really, and so on. Also, I threw in some extras about hydrogen fusion, solar flares, and the curvature of space-time around the sun. I may have also mentioned that it will burn out one day and all life on Earth will disappear forever.

If Mom was put off by my lecture on the lake, I was irked that she had brought God into it. By that time, I had abandoned the faith of my childhood. I hadn't crossed into outright atheism but had lost touch with the Christian God who created the universe and performed miracles and, in the words of my Baptist upbringing, lived in my heart. My belief was well expressed by these words of Albert Einstein: "I do not believe in a personal God. . . . If something is in me which can be called religious then it is the unbounded admiration for the structure of the world so far as our science can reveal it."[2] Maybe something like a mind was behind all of this, I figured. If so, its workings remained vague and remote. There was no way it knew my name.

How are we to see the sun and, by extension, the cosmos? On one hand, the sun glorifies God, bears the likeness of its creator, and stands as an unmistakable marker of God's presence and steadfastness and power. On the other hand, the sun fuses millions of tons of hydrogen into helium every second and stands as an inevitable product of an impersonal cosmos, a writhing nuclear dynamo blazing its way toward permanent gloom.

During high school and college, I thought I had to choose between these two options, and I chose science, which struck me as grown-up and real. Beside it, faith seemed childish and made-up, like a crutch for people who couldn't handle facts. God, I thought, was something you're supposed to believe in until you learn physics.

I no longer think this. In fact, I was already beginning to see things in a new way that evening on the lake, and my whole adult life has been lived out of a conviction that faith and science do not compete but instead complement one another. But it's worth pausing for a chapter to see why, as a high school and college student, I thought so very differently.

2.

I'm Pretty Sure My Life Was Changed by a Second-Grade Field Trip: The Problem Shows Up and Grows Up

Science first exploded into my consciousness the day I, along with other members of Midvale Elementary School's second-grade class, visited a place called Fernbank Science Center. There, we were welcomed by a display of stuffed native animals arranged in artificial habitats: black bears wading in glass water, a fox with raised foreleg focusing through glass eyes on a pair of huddled field mice, a Blue Ridge vista painted on the wall behind them. A hand-cranked model of a tornado and a Mercury-era space capsule stood around the corner, and a nature trail wound through the forest out back. But we had our sights set on Fernbank's main attraction: its planetarium.

We entered the circular hall and plopped into the low-slung chairs, wondering what would happen there. Curiously we regarded the room. A monstrous star projector stood in the center of the floor, swathed in blue light, humming softly. Four illuminated letters marking the cardinal directions—N, E, S, W—were set high in the circular wall. A vast onion-colored dome, divided into thin sections by pale lines, towered above us. These lines converged on the zenith, drawing all eyes upward to its nearly invisible height. The cavernous space and clean lines evoked a sense of awed reverence, like a sci-fi sanctuary.

We grew silent as the lights faded and the dome dimmed. Small points of light appeared—one, then two, then two dozen. As the darkness deepened, the stars shone brighter against it, and I was overcome by a happy, peaceful feeling. The slowly darkening sky and brightening stars made me feel suspended, as if I had left my seat behind. The dome seemed to draw closer as the light fell. I kept thinking the room could grow no darker, but the stars continued to multiply.

After what seemed like a very long time, the room finally achieved maximum darkness. Thousands of stars shone bright and hard against the inky dome. The narrator began to speak as the stars slowly revolved about some invisible axis. The planets and sun and moon wandered the lanes of the zodiac. Wonderstruck, I watched as great tilting gridlines and shining mythical figures emerged from the darkness, connecting the stars by number and story. Someone watching from a distance would have seen nothing but a boy reclining motionless under an artificial electronic sky, but my soul had found its home.

After this, I learned all the astronomy I could. From there, with Dad's help, I familiarized myself with the basics of evolution and natural history. I became the household dinosaur expert. My parents supported my obsession, buying me astronomy books and dinosaur books and a large collection of plastic tyrannosaurs and stegosaurs and apatosaurs. I slipped them into my pockets before leaving for school. At recess, I played with them on an outcrop of rock, which looked pretty prehistoric to me, at the far end of the playground.

Science Might Be a Problem for Jesus

Meanwhile, my parents took my siblings and me to church every time the doors opened, and over time, certain problems presented themselves to me. I was taught Bible stories that plainly conflicted with evolution. It seemed impossible to reconcile Genesis with what I had learned from my natural-history and dinosaur books.

Also, God had apparently created the world in a pretty bloody way. A picture from the last page of one of my natural-history books haunts me to this day. In it, a dry streambed runs from the hard, mountainous horizon to the foreground, where a half-starved saber-toothed tiger rides atop some doomed proto-mammal, digging its claws and teeth into it. The unfortunate creature gapes blankly up at a ceiling of low yellow clouds, having come looking for water but having found death instead.

I thought God should be at least as nice as my mom and dad, and they would never hurt any creature like this. But evolution is a long, messy business, and lots of animals and human beings have had to suffer over many millions of years to get us where we are today. Surely a loving God wouldn't spill so much blood just to make a world. Surely there would be another way.

Then there was the future to think about. It made me sad and scared to think that Earth and the life on it will not last forever, that one day the sun will run out of fuel and our green planet will be transformed into a dry and windless wasteland. I wondered how this squared with what I had been taught about heaven. The afterlife must exist in some other world, I reasoned, or some other dimension. As I progressed through my teen years, I thought to myself that maybe heaven isn't real at all. Maybe we made it up.

Maybe when we die, the lights will go out, and that will be it.

I learned how small and brief human life is when placed in a cosmic perspective, and this terrified me. We are specks of dust on a lonely planet in the outer reaches of a perfectly ordinary galaxy, here one instant, gone the next. But at church, I was taught that we are cosmically important—that we live and move at the very center of God's attention and love.

As the years went by, I began to think how science might be a problem for Jesus, or at least for certain beliefs about Jesus. How weird it was for anyone to believe in such antiscientific ideas as his virgin birth, his human and divine nature, and his resurrection! Also, all of the miracles of Jesus and the others in the Bible—the flood, the birth of Isaac, the parting of the sea, and so on—became problematic in the light of science.

Other problems arose as I learned more. History told me a natural conflict exists between science and religion. Galileo, for example, suffered at the hands of the church for saying that Earth travels around the sun. And this same conflict is evidenced by our ongoing religion-versus-science war; atheists say science disproves God, and they're always arguing with Christians who say evolution is wrong.

Taken together, these problems seemed insurmountable. The two points of view appeared flatly incompatible. But something deeper nagged me, something more troubling than mere inconsistency.

It Was Something to Do with Stacy

In youth Sunday school, while most of us were goofing off and half listening, my friend Stacy paid attention. Unsatisfied with the standard Southern Baptist explanations for nearly everything, she would regularly pop out questions like "Did God kill Jesus?" and "Didn't God know we would go bad?" and "Why does the Bible contradict itself?"

This made our teachers uncomfortable. They didn't know what to say, so they just sat in a fidgety silence, deferred to another teacher or to the pastor, resorted to clichés, or said something awkward or something that begged the question or something beside the point. The lesson I took from this was that church is no place to ask questions.

Now, this is not what happened whenever I asked science questions. Once I asked Dad how we knew Earth was so old. "The fossil record," he said. "Radiometric dating," he said. "Plate tectonics," he said. I didn't understand all of it, but answers are more than words. Here there was no anxiety. My questions actually made Dad *happy.* His manner told me that if I had further questions, I could always ask, and if he didn't know the answer, then maybe we could figure it out together.

So what I experienced was that asking questions about God and the Bible was not okay, but asking questions about science was okay and even fun. Science seemed open and easy, while religion seemed nervous and touchy. The folks at church loved me and were kind, but after a year or two of Stacy's questions, I began to wonder if they were trying to hide something. When it came time to head to college, I left my faith behind along with my childhood.

A Hard Problem

My faith eventually returned in a new form. That story will be told later, but for now we'll remain with the problem, summarized here:

- Reading Genesis 1 and 2 and other biblical passages at face value tells us the cosmos and everything in it was created over six twenty-four-hour periods about six thousand years ago, that a single human couple was created at that time, that animal kinds remain fixed and unchangeable, and that human beings were made special and apart from the animals.

  Science rejects all of this. It tells us the cosmos as we know it began with a great boom 13.8 billion years ago, that life on Earth has evolved over the last 3.5 billion, and that human beings are related to all living things. I mean this literally. If you trace your family back far enough, you'll find that you're descended not only from your great-great-grandparents and from apes long before them but also from small ratlike mammals. And if you keep going, you'll find weird, long-extinct lizards in your family line in addition to amphibians and fish and worms and sponges and single-celled organisms. These are your *ancestors*. Present-day housecats and narwhals and rotifers and *E. coli* and spiders and lichen and tardigrades and ferns and mushrooms and pipefish and hickory trees are your *relatives*.

  From a scientific point of view, human beings showed up several hundred thousand years ago as one of countless life forms that have populated the planet in its 4.5-billion-year history. And we're still changing. Evolution never sleeps. If, a million or so years from now, our descendants were to send a picture of themselves back in time to us, we'd not recognize them as human.

• Genesis declares we're made in the image of God. But science describes us as animals, as organisms within an environment, and has nothing to say about the divine image.

• Christianity and science paint different pictures of the future. Our faith tells us that our bodies will be resurrected one day and that we'll live in paradise with God and one another (however we might imagine that). Science informs us that the cosmos will eventually wind down into a permanent and frozen state of silence, darkness, and lifelessness.[1]

• The Christian faith tells us that human beings play a major role in the cosmos, but science disagrees. The size and age of the universe transcend our wildest imaginings. It's impossible to exaggerate this: we occupy an infinitesimal point in space and time. We do not live at the center of the universe; in fact, it has no center at all. Nor do we live at a special point in time.

• Scripture says that pain and suffering resulted from human sin, but science disagrees. Evolution runs on death, often painful and prolonged, and it got started long before we showed up. No distinction can be drawn between the history of life and the history of death.

    Of all the species that have ever existed, only

one in a thousand exist today. The fossil record shows that extinctions have come in waves, killing hundreds of thousands of species over short spans of time and, in most cases, for no known reason.

- Christianity is founded on miracles, but science casts doubt on all miracles.

- My understanding of history said that science and faith naturally oppose one another. Think of Galileo and his trouble with the church. The contemporary evolution-versus-creation debate reveals that this conflict continues today.

- In my experience, teachers of faith seemed touchy about questions, but teachers of science welcomed questions happily.

Such differences make us wonder how to think about the relationship between faith and science. They may even cause us to abandon hope of ever solving this problem.

It's a hard job. Both science and religion comprise vast, complex, and evolving beliefs and practices. They not only make claims about the world (e.g., "repent and you shall be saved," "the rings of Uranus are made of ice and dust"[2]) but also comprehend the world in distinct ways (e.g., divine revelation, controlled experiments). And these ways of knowing are practiced in separate communities, each with its own particular values and traditions.

The communities of faith and science are each composed of numerous sub-communities. For example, among the thousands of Christian sub-communities, you'll find such varied groups as the Society of Friends, the Roman Catholic Church, and the Antiochian Orthodox Church.[3] Among the hundreds of scientific sub-communities, you'll find the American Society of Ichthyologists and Herpetologists, the American Astronomical Society, and the Society for Electroanalytical Chemistry. Some of these sub-communities span the globe and contain countless sub-subgroups. In a dozen lifetimes, you couldn't possibly learn all there is to know about Christianity or science separately, and here we are trying to find a way to relate them.

Metaphors often help simplify such big, messy problems. For our current task, we'll imagine faith and science as two people and ask what kind of relationship they might share. We could imagine many kinds of relationships, but in the next chapter, we'll focus on faith and science as enemies, and in the following one, the two as strangers, friends, and partners in marriage.[4]

3.

How Not to Chessbox: Faith and Science Face Off

You've probably never heard of Ruthie Ann Wright or Jenny-Anne Dexter. Wright lectures at the University of Exeter, and Dexter works at a British children's charity. Mostly they have nothing to do with each other, but on October 18, 2012, for an hour or so, they were locked in battle. On that day, they went head-to-head for the first British women's chessboxing championship.

Yes, chessboxing. It's exactly what it sounds like. A match consists of eleven rounds, six of chess and five of boxing. It begins with chess, switches to boxing, then back to chess, and so on, ending with chess. Started by a Dutch performance artist in 2003, it quickly gained legitimacy. Today chessboxers have established several global organizations, and the sport has become quite popular in parts of Europe and Asia.

Chessboxing attracts those who value *total* competition. The whole person—body and mind—gets involved. Not content to simply box or play chess, chessboxers do it all. If all boxers were content to box and all chess players were content to play chess, they would never square up against each other. But chessboxers do everything, so they battle it out as enemies.

Making a Mess of It

Sometimes faith and science act like a couple of chess-boxers. If faith were content to play its traditional role of connecting us with God and providing ethical and spiritual direction, it would never square off against science. And if science were content to explore the cosmos, extend life spans, and build better mousetraps, it would never compete against faith. But sometimes both characters insist on doing everything, and when this happens, they become like Wright and Dexter: enemies, locked in battle.

The trouble is, unlike Wright and Dexter, they both make a mess of it.

For a good example of faith making a mess of it, look no further than Grant County, Kentucky, where a full-scale replica of Noah's ark houses animatronic dinosaurs for the wonderment and education of the paying public. "Since dinosaurs were land animals, and God made all the land animals on day six of the creation week, dinosaurs were created on day six. Therefore dinosaurs lived with people . . . and went on board Noah's Ark," writes Ken Ham, founder and CEO of Answers in Genesis, the organization responsible for the attraction.[1] He claims that the cosmos and everything in it was created over six twenty-four-hour periods about six thousand years ago and that a flood covered the entire planet about 4,400 years ago. For support, he enlists the Bible, which he views as a factual historical document to be read and understood in its plainest, most physical sense.

Creationists like Ham look to faith to do all the stuff it has always done, like provide moral direction and teach us about our relationship with God. But they also give faith the job of determining which scientific ideas to accept and which to reject. Like a boxer playing chess, they put faith to the task of doing science.

Ham accepts gravity and atomic physics and certain aspects of cell biology, for example, but rejects the big bang and evolution and other established scientific ideas that contradict his understanding of the Bible. But science, a single tapestry woven of interconnected ideas, is not so easily taken apart. Once these theories and other foundational concepts in astronomy, geology, biology, and physics are removed, nothing remains of science but a few unconnected scraps and threads.

In addition to slicing science down to nothing, this view turns God into a fraud. Who but a swindler would create a six-thousand-year-old universe that, no matter how closely we look, no matter how we approach the problem, and no matter what theories or observations we employ, appears to be 13.8 billion years old? This scientific consensus is the product of centuries of cautious and critical and coordinated work performed by some of the most intelligent and dedicated human beings on the planet. If the universe really was created six thousand years ago, we are forced to conclude that it was meticulously crafted to throw us off the trail.

Faith shouldn't stand opposed to humanity's best knowledge about the biological and physical world. When it does, it shrinks itself down to a set of rigid and empty beliefs that bear no relation to the heart of Scripture or to the actual cosmos. Dinosaurs on the ark, science in shreds, and a fraud on the divine throne—this is what happens when religion, the native boxer, decides to play chess also.

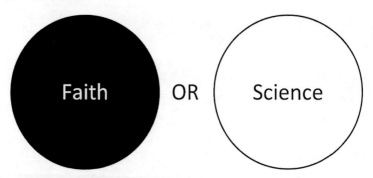

Enemies: One wins and the other loses. They cannot exist in harmony.

English Teachers against Atheists

When science lines up against faith, it makes its own mess. Seeing that the evidence contradicts a plain reading of Genesis, many scientists reject faith altogether. Super-famous atheist and biologist Richard Dawkins, in his book *The Blind Watchmaker*, wrote, "Nearly all peoples have developed their own creation myth, and the Genesis story is just the one that happened to have been adopted by one particular tribe of Middle Eastern herders. It has no more special status than the belief of a particular West African tribe that the world was created from the excrement of ants."[2] I don't know what Dawkins has against West African tribes and ant poop, but I think it's safe to say that if Genesis had lined up nicely with modern science, he would not write it off so quickly.

Dawkins, like all scientists, demands that data be as self-consistent and logically complete as possible. But unlike many scientists, he treats *the Bible* like a data set. This is evidenced by the fact that his website links to an infographic called "Contradictions in the Bible," an online resource that presents every logical contradiction found in Scripture in a brilliant visual format. It's beautifully done and fun to look at.[3]

There is, of course, a larger point. "Contradictions" was originally created by the Reason Project, a group headed by Sam Harris, another well-known atheist who has zero patience with faith of any kind. The infographic makes a powerful visual argument: since the Bible contains so many contradictions, Christianity cannot be true.

Many of the contradictions make no theological difference. For example, one refers to the volume of the *molten sea*, a large basin for the ritual washing of priests, located in the inner court of Solomon's Temple. The passage from 1 Kings 7:26 states that the molten sea "held two thousand baths," while 2 Chronicles 4:5 says it held three thousand.

Others display an ignorance of literary devices that would enrage any middle-school English teacher. For example, Psalm 44 finds a frustrated and despondent Israel crying out to God, "Rouse yourself! Why do you sleep, O Lord? Awake, do not cast us off forever" (v. 23), yet Psalm 121 reminds us that "He who keeps Israel will neither slumber nor sleep" (v. 4). You'll count this as a contradiction only if you believe the psalmist is using the word *sleep* in a literal way and believes in a God who actually sleeps as human beings do.

Treating Scripture this way does little to dismantle any but the flimsiest of religious beliefs, because the value of Scripture does not lie in its use as a scientific data set. Its power is located in its deep currents, its poetry, and its connection with humanity's most profound experiences and hopes and loves. Nonetheless, many scientifically motivated atheists miss this point. Thinking such arguments put faith on the ropes, they try for a knockout.

They do this by making science do all the stuff faith normally does, like providing moral direction and a sense of meaning. In his book *The Moral Landscape*, Harris looks to neuroscience to tell us the "right and wrong answers to questions of human values."[4] Meanwhile, on Dawkins's website, Professor Gleb Tsipursky writes that psychology and cognitive neuroscience make it possible for "science to fill that emptiness deep in the pit of our stomach that comes from a lack of a personal sense of meaning and purpose. We can use science to answer the question 'what is the meaning of life?'"[5]

Like a chess player trying to apply the rules of that game to boxing, science is ill equipped for this task and so makes a mess of it. No matter how hard it tries to do otherwise, science is capable of revealing only what is, not what should be. But as the enemy of faith, science rejects that distinction and says, "I do everything, including morality and meaning." Scripture reduced to a data set, language drained of meaning, and science overburdened with impossible tasks—this is what happens when science, the native chess player, decides to box also.

If you seek simple and unrealistic answers to difficult problems, this option might be for you. But if you want to go deeper into both faith *and* science, you'll look elsewhere, and I recommend you start with the next chapter.

4.

Strangers, Friends, Lovers: Cooperation, Not Competition

I reside in a rather large city among people with whom I have nothing in common besides the obvious fact that we're living in the same city at the same time. Our lives don't overlap. Their presence cheers me, of course. I am pro-person. But I hold no *particular* affection for them. They live in their neighborhoods, and I live in mine. They do their jobs, and I do mine. They have their friends, and I have mine. And nobody, apparently, feels a need to change this state of affairs.

Perhaps faith and science also live in separate neighborhoods, work separate jobs, and lead separate lives. Maybe each performs its own tasks and pursues its own interests, happy for the other's existence but uninterested in manufacturing a relationship where there is none. Perhaps faith and science are strangers.

Several years ago, I was driving my son, Henry, through our neighborhood in our Honda. He asked about Genesis and evolution and how they could both be right (we talk about this more than the average family). "Consider our car," I said. "We can ask different questions about it. We can ask *who* made it (the Japanese), *why* it was made (for transportation), and *how* it was made (with computers and robots). These different questions have different answers, and we have no problem keeping them separated."

"In the same way," I said, "faith and science address different questions. The Bible tells us *who* created the universe (God) and *why* the world was made (because God is creative and loving), and science tells us *how* it was done (big bang, evolution, etc.)."[1]

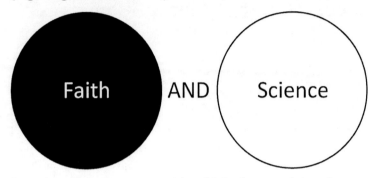

Strangers: There is no competition. It's both one and the other. They exist in harmony by not overlapping.

Or think of it another way: science tells us what the universe is like, and faith tells us how we should live. The late Harvard biologist Stephen Jay Gould wrote, "Science covers the empirical universe: what it is made of and why does it work this way. Religion extends over questions of moral meaning and value. These two do not overlap. . . . Science gets the age of rocks, and religion retains the rock of ages; science studies how the heavens go, and religion determines how to go to heaven."[2]

This view is held by many science teachers. Students and parents often claim that evolution violates their religious beliefs. But evolution is basic science and must be taught (although, in fact, about 60 percent of public high school biology teachers cut corners when they get to the topic).[3] But if faith and science live as strangers, no overlap occurs, and teachers are set free to teach evolution, which does not—in fact, cannot—impinge on religious beliefs.

Suppose I held up a grapefruit and asked you, "Is this fruit yellow or spherical?" You would say the question makes no sense. "Yellow" and "spherical" have nothing to do with each other. They're independent qualities. You could have a yellow non-spherical fruit (like a banana) or a non-yellow spherical fruit (like an orange). Though independent, the color yellow and the spherical shape work alongside one another to make the grapefruit what it is.

Similarly, the theological term *creation* implies a relationship between the Creator and the creation, while the scientific term *evolution* implies that certain kinds of observations have been made and certain kinds of evidence have been gathered. Though independent, creation and evolution work alongside one another to make the world what it is.

As strangers, science and faith get along by minding their own business. They live and let live. This simple, commonsense approach appeals to the peacekeeping instincts of people everywhere: why fight?

Faith and Science in the Corner Booth

Now suppose faith and science meet. Perhaps they're standing in the same checkout line at Target or they're seated in adjacent booths at a restaurant. Maybe they show up at the same party.

What happens next? Well, what happens when *you* meet someone new? You ask questions. You ask where they're from or where they go to school or if they have any siblings. You look for common ground. This is what faith and science do, too, and they find some. In fact, they hit it off and decide to meet for coffee.

At the coffee bar, they take a corner booth and promptly discover that they've both been misunderstood. This leads to a fabulous conversation (few things bring people together more quickly than shared grievance). For its part, science complains that everyone thinks it's always super-objective and universal, the final word on everything.

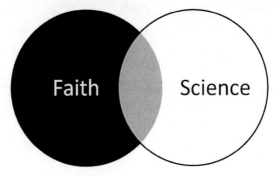

Friends: There are distinct differences but no real competition. Faith and science exist in harmony and have some points of common interest but ultimately go their own ways.

"People think I show the whole world exactly, precisely as it is," science complains. "But I see through my own lenses. I do not provide unbiased and complete information about all things. I ask and answer only certain kinds of questions. I do not stand outside the world. I am part of it and share its messiness and uncertainty."

"I'm misunderstood also," says faith. "So many people think I depend only on private and personal and touchy-feely emotions! It drives me bananas. I, too, live in this world and am as likely to see it clearly as anyone else. I, too, have methods and norms. I, too, am shaped by reality. I am at my best when I engage the world as it is, just like you."

"I begin in wonder," says science on another day. "I was born on the day we looked up and saw that we live in a cosmos not of our making. I grew up as we learned how we came to be here and what the cosmos is like. And the more we learn, the greater the mystery of existence becomes.

Solving scientific problems does not solve this mystery; it deepens it."

"Yes!" replies faith. "My path also starts in wonder. I, too, am astounded by the fact of existence. I also want to know how we got here and why. I mean, really! We just showed up! Nobody asked us, did they? It's amazing, and I share your deep need to make sense of the world. My questions lead me in a different direction—I want to know how to live and what the purpose of life is—but wonder is my starting point, and wonder motivates me still."

They have more in common. For example, science raises ethical questions that join it to faith—think about antidepressants, carbon emissions, and genetic editing. They also share assumptions about the order and structure of the universe, and so on. To put it most simply, faith and science discover that they live in the same universe. Jesus of Nazareth and *T. rex* walked on the same planet and, on an evolutionary scale, at nearly the same time. Once you begin looking closely, you'll see that the idea of faith and science as strangers is too simple.

They have a great time and plenty of laughs but feel no pressure to take their relationship beyond a casual and mutually rewarding friendship. They don't try to be BFFs. Romance never enters the picture. They just hang out whenever they can, and when they leave the coffee bar, they go home in different directions to their own neighborhoods and jobs, knowing they will meet again. They move forward enlightened by, but not alongside, one another.

One Flesh

Sometimes you meet someone and the world lights up. You are comforted by your similarities and exhilarated by your differences. You get along so well that you can't imagine moving forward without one another. Sometimes a relationship bears so much fruit that to end it would be folly, and both parties know it.

Suppose science and faith meet, and they hit it off completely. Their common roots in wonder, parallel paths toward understanding, and mutual illumination make theirs a relationship worth protecting and extending as long as both parties endure. Their alliance is grounded in a mutual search for truth and animated by their outward differences. So they take the plunge. They fall in love, get married, and in the words of Jesus, become one flesh.

This perspective is most commonly expressed in two kinds of theology. The first, *natural theology,* looks not to the Bible or Christian tradition but to reason and nature and science for clues about the character of God. It's similar to something we do all the time: learn about someone by considering the things they create.

Consider Georgia O'Keeffe; her flowers and skulls reflect her fascination with the duality of life and death. The music of Bach reveals the composer's orderly mind. Anyone who listens to Bruno Mars knows he loves fashion, dancing, and contemporary urban culture. In the same way, we might learn something about the Creator by examining the creation. Science then becomes a search for clues about God, an investigation of the divine nature.

Faithnscience

Partners in marriage: There really is no distinction between them.

Process theology attempts a complete synthesis of science and Christianity. This is a deeply philosophical approach that completely reworks Christianity in the light of modern science, a melding of the two into a single conceptual system. It rejects the traditional belief known as *divine omnipotence*, meaning that God can do anything at all. It claims among other things that God can create only with the cooperation of creatures, that God is not in complete control of the universe, and that Jesus was not *essentially* different from any other human being, just more deeply connected to God.

All three perspectives outlined here—strangers, friends, and partners in marriage—emphasize cooperation over competition. The last two go further, claiming that faith and science have something constructive to say to one another and that their relationship has the potential to bear fruit. Even so, a problem arises. All three maintain that faith and science share a common status, like two fundamentally equal human beings. But faith and science do not stand on equal footing. We will see how this is, and how either science will come to rule faith or faith will come to encompass science, in the next chapter.

5.

A Universe with a Point: How Science Enlarges Faith

I stepped from the dim confines of Building 2 out into the blinding midday. The sprawling campus of NASA's Goddard Space Flight Center lay parched and exhausted around me. After catching my breath (July in Maryland feels a lot like July in Georgia), I stood still for a moment, absorbing the shock of heat and light. A gaggle of Canada geese wandered the goose-poop-dappled sidewalk along Delta Road. Nothing else moved. Satellite dishes sagged atop low structures. Automobiles stood in silent rows, baking. I could almost hear the weeds dying. I turned my face up to the sun, smiled broadly, and shoved off on a two-mile victory walk.

I had just received an email from a colleague in Brazil. "Great news!" he wrote. "The optical source shows clear variable polarization. This confirms our quasar identification." This message marked the end of my yearlong effort to identify an unusual source of gamma rays at the eastern edge of Sagittarius. Yes, gamma rays—the radiation that transformed Bruce Banner into the Hulk—stream down constantly from the sky.[1] My source turned out to be a quasar, a remote and luminous galaxy in its early stages of formation, powered by the gravitational energy of a supermassive black hole. At the time, very few quasars were known to emit gamma rays, making my discovery note-worthy.

I sidestepped my way along Explorer Road toward God-dard's back entrance, avoiding goose poop and basking in the satisfaction of having solved a scientific puzzle. Gamma-ray quasars have a four-part signature, and until that day, I had confirmed three for the Sagittarius source. My colleague's measurement of variable optical polariza-tion—the fourth—snapped the lid on the project, and a new item appeared in the storehouse of human knowledge.

For my part, I sensed an immediate personal connection with a galaxy billions of light-years distant and moving away at well more than half the speed of light. Before being intercepted by NASA's orbiting telescope, gamma rays from this quasar had traveled at the fastest possible speed for seven billion years. During this time, the distant galaxy had surely evolved into something like the Milky Way even as it receded farther and faster into the cosmic distance. This may sound abstract and mysterious to you, but to me, it was as concrete as the sidewalk under my feet. I felt that I myself had somehow spanned the universe. Rarely have I felt so grounded and happy.

The experience reminded me of my time as a researcher in a nuclear lab. Atomic nuclei compare well to quasars for their mystery and abstraction. They surround us—they *are* us—but, like quasars, require great effort to investigate and imagine. Looking deep into matter and discovering new details of atomic nuclei made me feel no less connected to the cosmos than investigating galaxies billions of light-years distant. The whole evolving universe, from the tini-est ghostlike particles through the panorama of earthly life to the grandest cosmic structures, emerged in one seamless vision in my mind's eye as I wound across Goddard's sun-baked campus.

I returned to Building 2 and began the happy work of writing up my discovery for publication. Later I reemerged into the swelter, left Goddard on foot, and walked to our nearby studio apartment, where I found my wife, Elizabeth, and one-year-old son, Henry, ready to venture into Washington for a celebration dinner.

We returned hours later, sleepy and full. Elizabeth and I were full, anyway; Henry was weaning and had not yet had his bottle, so I fed him. I sat in the dark nursery, holding him and the warm bottle and watching his eyelids droop as he drank. By the time he finished, he was nearly unconscious. I placed him in his crib and watched him settle peaceably into his favorite belly-down fetal position and drop into sleep.

Again I felt at home, grounded, happy beyond description. Just as I had on my walk, I sensed a connection to the world beyond me. But this was neither quasar nor nucleus; it was my son. I was overcome by the most common of loves—that of a parent for a child, as real and immeasurable as the universe itself. Lost in wonder, I stood watching him sleep. After a moment, I left him, and one of the happiest days of my life came to a close.

A Thin Quantum Mist

I can still see the scientific vision that emerged during my victory walk on that hot Maryland day. Quarks were buzzing at the very roots of matter, and frenzied atoms combined into long molecules of DNA within cell nuclei. Algae were blooming in tropical waters as great migrations of birds were crossing the globe. Jupiter's Great Red Spot was churning; stars were cycling through their lives, dying in radiant showers of hydrogen and helium and carbon ions; and galaxies were colliding. And 13.8 billion years of cosmic evolution were drawing it all together into a single brilliant tapestry flowing with life and light and energy.

In the face of this vision, however, I admit that I experienced a certain emptiness. Science cultivates wonder and fills my mind but leaves my heart stranded in the midst of a vast and alien dance. What's more, the more science I learn, the more adrift I feel. I cannot see how I fit into such a vision, or how Henry fits in, or how love fits in.

I can see how Henry and I fit in *biologically*: we live as organisms within an environment, related to all life. And what we call love may very well help preserve our genes and keep *Homo sapiens* from extinction. In this way, we and love certainly fit in. But within a purely scientific view, we are no more than organisms, and our moral impulse to love evaporates into survival mechanisms and patterns of neurons firing fast in our heads and, in turn, into quarks and other elementary particles transferring energy to one another according to mathematical laws and, in turn, into what? Smaller particles? Eleven-dimensional vibrating strings? The deeper we look, the more elusive the world becomes, and love, so real and central to us human creatures, vaporizes into a thin quantum mist.

These explanations have their place. If science offers an account of life and love, we are wrong to dismiss it outright. Such an account fails to satisfy, however, because what science tears apart it alone cannot put together again. The words of Nobel Prize–winning physicist Steven Weinberg come to mind: "The more the universe seems comprehensible, the more it also seems pointless."[2]

Inside Information

But not a single one of us inhabits a world without a point. None of us has lived a single meaning-free moment. Even experiences of meaninglessness point to this truth, for it is out of our craving for meaning that such feelings arise. We continually think and speak and write and act on the basis of values like love. Questions of purpose and meaning (what should be) occur to us at least as often, and nearly always more urgently, as questions of science (what is). We are bound to morality and driven by love, the greatest of Christian virtues.

And love goes far beyond the affection of a father for his young son. Love motivates our everyday moral choices but also inspires heroic acts of selflessness and justice. Think of Oskar Schindler, a member of the Nazi Party who risked his life for the lives of 1,200 Jews during the Holocaust. Think of Rosa Parks, who remained in her seat on a Montgomery bus in 1955, igniting the first major direct-action campaign of the civil-rights movement. Think of James Harrison, an Aussie who donated his unique antibody-laden blood once a week for sixty years, thereby saving 2.4 *million* lives.

Do these choices matter? Are they significant? Of course they are.

But a purely scientific vision of the universe contradicts this, offering us nothing in the way of motivation or justification when it comes to our moral choices. Nowhere in that vision do I find help loving Henry and my other children—which is rarely as easy as it was that evening in Maryland—or making difficult ethical choices. Love and justice and other values are not waiting to be discovered out there somewhere like some new class of quasar. They are inside information, found within the hearts and minds of creatures called human beings. And you don't need to know anything about genetics or astrophysics or chemistry or Jupiter's Great Red Spot to understand and act according to these words of Martin Luther King Jr.: "The arc of the moral universe is long, but it bends toward justice."[3] No such arc can be found within the world of science.

When Weinberg writes, "The more the universe seems comprehensible, the more it also seems pointless," he is talking about *scientific* comprehension. He is talking about physics. He is talking about what you see when you look at the world through the lenses of science. Once you realize this, his claim no longer seems depressing. It becomes a simple statement about science, which, like sunglasses blocking certain wavelengths of light, filters out all notions of meaning and purpose and values before it even gets started. It considers only what is and not what should be. So it comes as no surprise that the universe appears pointless when Weinberg—or when I on my victory walk or when anyone else—surveys it through the lenses of science.

Some hard-boiled materialists might claim that Darwin-style survival counts as a fine purpose, and that we should value the choices of Schindler and Parks and Harrison and the oratory of MLK because they increase our long-term chances. Again, science provides no basis for this claim. It says we admire these choices only because our biology happened to develop such that it demands our admiration for them. It suggests that human morality has evolved as a side effect, amplified over thousands of generations, that helps our species survive one more. It, like everything else, has appeared in the universe accidentally and without significance.

Two Roads

Two roads diverge before us. Down the first, we are freaks, moral creatures coughed up by an amoral universe, saddled by evolution with this heavy load, this unshakable sense of value, this obsession with meaning, doomed to live out our short and difficult lives in a cosmos that doesn't care about us or our choices. Better to be an amoeba or cat or maple tree, unburdened by such troubles. We may endure a while. We may colonize the solar system or even the Milky Way, but all things will eventually wind down in the face of endless cold and infinite time. The universe will not be tamed. It will swallow us.

Down the second road, our morality and sense of values reveal something as actual and fundamental as energy, time, space, and light. We belong in the universe no less than electrons and quasars, and we simply cannot stop living our lives as if love is real and as if it matters ultimately. So maybe it *is* real and *does* matter ultimately. We are not freaks. Instead, we express a core cosmic reality when, guided by love and justice, we make even the tiniest of choices. We are drawn by love toward a world we can't quite see but occasionally glimpse whenever an Oskar Schindler or a Rosa Parks or a James Harrison shows up, a world envisioned and described by Martin Luther King Jr., a world Jesus called the kingdom of God.[4]

I walk the second road out of a desire for integrity, which means wholeness. It means to be of one mind, consistent in thought and action. I cannot live as if my choices and actions matter while believing or even suspecting that they do not. We must line up our beliefs about the world with our experience of the world and our deeds in it. Like good scientists who wish to remain connected to reality, we must adjust our theory to the data.

Your Daddy Was a Film of Chemical Slime

You may join Steven Weinberg as he walks the first road or me as I walk the second, but science will not help you choose. An illustration will demonstrate this. Consider one of the most powerful and traditional images of God: that of Father. Jesus used this image all the time, perhaps most memorably in the parable of the prodigal son (Luke 15:11–32), in which God is represented as a father of two sons.

The younger son asks for his full inheritance early, and the father gives it to him. Immediately the boy leaves home, squanders the money on fleeting and shallow pleasures, and ends up with nothing. Even pig food begins to look good to him. He eventually comes to his senses and returns to his father, who, instead of punishing him or turning his back in silence or putting him to work as a servant, welcomes him home with a joyful embrace and an all-night party.

This story tells us we are each loved by God, just as the prodigal was loved by his father.

Not everyone agrees, and some look to science to make their point. P. Z. Myers, biologist and traveler of the first road, has this to say about the heavenly father:

> You don't have a heavenly father at all. You're a mediocre product of a wasteful and entirely impersonal process. We've done the paternity tests. We are apes and the descendants of apes, who were the descendants of rat-like primates, who were the children of reptiles, who were the spawn of amphibians, who were the terrestrial progeny of fish, who came

from worms, who were assembled from single-celled microorganisms, who were the products of chemistry. Your daddy was a film of chemical slime on a Hadean rock, and he didn't care about you—he was only obeying the laws of thermodynamics.[5]

Though his basic outlook matches up with Weinberg's and that of other scientific materialists, Myers is not a typical atheist. His language and theatrics tend toward extremes, and he veers into overstatement more often than his peers. I quote him not because he represents all atheists but to point out that while his assertion is consistent with science, as a whole it is not forced on him by science.

To demonstrate this, I offer this rewrite of Myers's paragraph:

You have a heavenly father. You're an amazing product of his ongoing creation project. We've discovered a lot about that project, which has been going on for billions of years. We are human beings, the descendants of apes, who were drawn from earlier, smaller primates. Our lineage also includes reptiles and amphibians and fish and worms and even single-celled organisms. Like a flower that grows from the dirt yet is not itself dirt, we have been gradually assembled out of chaotic and disorganized elements. You were formed from the dust of the ground, given the breath of life, and carry the image of a loving and creative Father who is crazy about you.

Which one do you choose? You may vote for Myers's scenario or mine, but be clear about this: *no scientific experiment or observation can distinguish between them.* These statements differ only in what is *not* scientific about them. I go further with the nonscientific stuff, but Myers, by throwing in words like "mediocre" and phrases like "he didn't care about you," contributes his own bits of non-science as well.

Myers's statement accounts for some facts: we have evolved from a progression of ever-more-complex life forms; we are built out of the same chemical elements as apes and amphibians and fish and *Salmonella* and every other living thing; all life is related. But it fails to account for the fact that there have appeared in the cosmos creatures who are thoroughly, irreducibly, and essentially moral in nature. Creatures like me, who, when they survey the cosmos scientifically, grow depressed and anxious at the meaninglessness of it all. Creatures like Weinberg, who, despite insisting that the universe is pointless, live as though it is not. In other words, a purely scientific vision of the cosmos cannot be squared with our lives as they are actually lived.

The faith-and-science diagram for those who travel the first road looks like this:

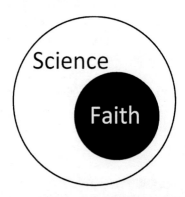

Science stands alone, the one reliable means of knowing anything at all. It describes the world objectively, universally, and finally. It reveals what can be known about religious faith no less than it reveals what can be known about galaxies, rainbows, and whales. Its explanations cover all there is to know. Walkers of the first road attribute all moral values and religious beliefs and practices to our particular (and pointless) evolutionary background, so the faith circle has been reduced in size to fit within science, which has retained its original size.[6]

When science rules faith, it reduces faith to science.

Introducing Science-Plus

If we call the first road *science*, we might call the second *science-plus*. Its diagram looks like this:

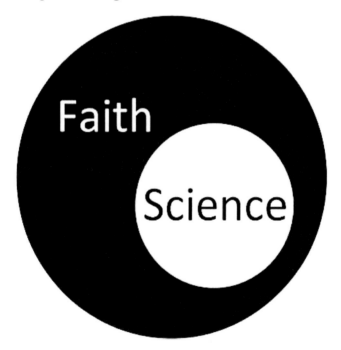

Science retains its original size, but faith has been enlarged to contain it. This doesn't mean that science should be taken over by faith communities or that the methods of faith should be substituted for the methods of science. You can't learn about matter-antimatter asymmetry or plate tectonics or horizontal gene transfer by reading the Bible. Faith is not a prerequisite for learning or doing science. The framing of experiments, the planning and execution of observations, and the collection and analysis of data stand apart from some of the more obvious aspects of faith such as worship, prayer, and Bible study.

But a grown-up, expanded faith shines a sacred light on all knowledge and all activities, even the most mundane, including science. As any student or scientist will tell you, the doing of science can grow tiresome and repetitive. Boredom often fills the long, long spaces between *a-ha* moments (the same can be said of the practice of faith).

But boredom is not the enemy; meaninglessness is. Memorizing the Krebs cycle and sifting through terabytes of astronomical data may appear to be secular and Godless activities, but that is an illusion enabled by a faith small enough to leave at church or in the privacy of your home. Mature faith expands to contain your whole life and even, as we shall see, the whole cosmos.

Your faith can expand until it's large enough to encompass science but humble enough to not restrict it. By allowing science to remain full-size, faith can transform science into a sacred task and the cosmos into a cathedral. You may not grow shiny and float on a cloud of good vibes as you read about Darwin's finches or fire up the proton accelerator, but your work will be accomplished and your whole life lived in a universe with a point.

The rest of this book is committed to showing you how to do this.

6.

A Larger, Stranger God: How Science Expands Your View of God

Fabulous stories had a way of springing up around Tycho Brahe, the last great European astronomer to never use a telescope. Happily for us, many of them were recorded.

He had superstitions about rabbits and old ladies. If either one crossed his path, he would return home immediately and remain indoors for the rest of the day. In 1566, his nose was sliced off in a swordfight. The duel with another Danish nobleman was not fought over a woman or a political point but over who was the better mathematician. For the rest of his life, Tycho[1] kept a small collection of metal replacement noses in a box; different occasions called for different noses. He owned a pet moose that met an unlikely end when it got drunk on beer and fell down a long flight of castle stairs. Tycho and his entourage, including a clairvoyant dwarf named Jepp, lived on a private island complete with a paper mill, a printing press, and a prison for unruly serfs (he had serfs). He entertained a constant stream of nobility and royalty, who came to feast at his table and gape at the wonders of Uraniborg, his over-the-top combination palace, research center, observatory, and alchemy lab located at the center of the island.[2]

Sensitive to social niceties, Tycho observed the fine points of etiquette at all times and died as a result of his scruples. Refusing to rise from a society dinner before the host, he held his urine so long that he developed a bladder infection. Complications of this infection led to the great astronomer's untimely death in October 1601. The telescope was invented seven years later.

Tycho never accepted Nicholas Copernicus's idea, proposed decades earlier, that Earth moves around the sun. He had many reasons for rejecting it. Contrary to popular belief, Copernicus had proved nothing, and Tycho knew it.[3] Anyone could see that Earth stood solid underfoot. Moreover, a moving Earth violated the physics of the day. No great wind blew as it would if Earth were turning; objects thrown straight up did not land to the west as they should; and the stars failed to display a tiny annual wobble, called *parallax*, that could have confirmed its motion. These arguments made Copernicus's theory preposterous to Tycho and to all but a few of his fellow astronomers.[4]

But Tycho's greatest problems with Copernicus had nothing to do with science. They concerned God, in at least two ways. The first related to the wholesale rearrangement of a cosmic scheme that was not only physical but theological. For centuries, humanity had seen itself as toiling near the lowest reaches of the cosmos while the Lord ruled serenely from his (and I do mean *his*; God was definitely male) throne far above the stars, atop all things. This towering cosmic model, on display most famously in Dante's *Divine Comedy*, provided a fitting setting for the human-divine drama of medieval Christianity. So what could it mean for Earth, whose fixed place in the cosmic basement had for centuries made both scientific and religious sense, to be raised high above the sun and set in motion? It confused the relationship between God and humanity, with no hard scientific evidence to back it up.

Another consequence of a sun-centered cosmos kept Tycho up at night, and it offended him more than the overall planetary reshuffling. It was this: if Earth moved around the sun as Copernicus had suggested, the distances to the stars would have to be *enormously* greater than Tycho believed (the reason has to do with the lack of stellar wobble, or parallax, mentioned above). If Copernicus were right, an incomprehensibly vast ocean of nothing at all would necessarily extend between the highest planet—Saturn at the time—and the stars. The distance would stretch to *at least* seven hundred times larger than Tycho preferred, and the universe would have to contain well more than three hundred *million* times the volume previously supposed.[5] This radical expansion of scale bothered Tycho profoundly. "Why would God have created so much empty space?" he asked, and in the end stated that, even if there had been no other absurdities to the Copernican theory, this alone would be sufficient to rule it out forever.[6]

Well, Copernicus's absurdities prevailed, and we may conclude that God did not make the world the way Tycho might have: centered on human beings, of a reasonable size, and in accordance with common sense. Apparently, Tycho believed God was more or less like him—human, efficient, reasonable—and should make a universe more or less the way he would. This theological belief led Tycho to reject one of the most influential and successful theories in the history of science. He resisted a larger, stranger universe because he resisted a larger, stranger God.

At the Beach with Alpha Centauri

The world has moved on since Tycho's time, and so has our understanding of the cosmos. His empty space has grown drastically, and today his argument—that God would not create so much emptiness—seems quaint. It draws from us little more than a bemused smile. But I suspect there's a bit of Tycho in each of us. Perhaps we smile because we know he was wrong and not because we've carefully considered the nature of the problem and found his point to be wholly out of place.

In 1833, a Scot named Thomas Henderson was named the director of the Royal Observatory in South Africa, where the bright triple star Alpha Centauri wheels high overhead all year round.[7] Henderson began measuring its position, along with those of other prominent southern stars, on a regular basis, and he found that Alpha Centauri wobbled back and forth a little once every year. This effect, the very parallax sought by Tycho, cannot be perceived by the naked eye but is as real and regular as the seasons. To Henderson, it revealed the star's distance, which he calculated to be nearly twenty trillion miles, six hundred times farther than Tycho's Copernicus-inspired worst-case nightmare scenario. Henderson, we now know, shorted this number; Alpha Centauri, the sun's closest stellar neighbor, lies about six trillion miles farther still.

Let's consider this distance in relation to the solar system. If the sun were shrunk down to basketball size and placed at the base of the Washington Monument in Washington, DC, Earth would be represented by a peppercorn eighty feet away. A blueberry at a distance of about sixteen hundred feet, at the near edge of the Lincoln Memorial Reflecting Pool, would serve nicely as Uranus. The entire solar system would fit within the limits of the National Mall, including Pluto and many comets that spend most of their time far beyond the orbit of Neptune.

On this scale, Henderson's star would not reside inside the city limits of Washington, DC, nor would it sit anywhere within the greater metropolitan area. In fact, it would

not be found in the states of Virginia or Maryland, nor anywhere in the eastern United States, nor would any point
within the whole continental United States be far enough
away. On our sun-as-a-basketball scale, the two brightest
stars of Alpha Centauri, our very closest, nearest-neighbor
star system, would be represented by a beach ball and a
bowling ball lying about sixteen hundred feet apart—the
same as the distance between the basketball sun and blueberry Uranus—on a beach on the Big Island of Hawaii. The
third star, a red dwarf called Proxima Centauri, lies nearer
to us than the others. In our scale model, it would be represented by a golf ball floating about two hundred miles off
the east coast of Hawaii—and yes, I'm aware that golf balls
do not float.

Larger, Faster

After Henderson, telescopes continued to grow larger, and
observing techniques continued to be refined. Every new
measurement pushed our cosmic horizon further away. No
matter how hard we searched for the edge of the universe,
we could not find it.

In 1924, an unexpected discovery re-upped the cosmic
distance scale many thousands of times. Astronomer
Edwin Hubble showed that our own Milky Way Galaxy,
itself many thousands of times farther across than the distance between Earth and Alpha Centauri, floats among an
uncountable number of other galaxies. The human imagination fails utterly when faced with the distances between
these galaxies. Spaces between planets are marked in light-
hours; those between stars are measured in light-years;
individual galaxies span thousands of light-years; and the
empty gulfs between adjacent galaxies stretch well into the

millions of light-years.[8] God, it seems, has opted to create on an incomprehensible and inhuman scale.

If this is insufficient to make us wonder about the intentions and character of the Creator, consider this: the universe itself is expanding. Using the hundred-inch telescope at Mount Wilson, California, Hubble demonstrated in 1929 that distances to remote galaxies are growing daily. The farther away the galaxy, the faster it's sailing away from us.

Much later, in 1999, it was discovered that this cosmic expansion, long assumed to be slowing down, is actually speeding up. Distant galaxies are not only moving away from us; they're moving away from us faster every day. The universe is not only growing larger every day; it's growing larger *faster* every day.[9]

You may ask, "Where are these galaxies going? Where's the edge of the universe? Where do the galaxies end?" The answer is "Nowhere." First, the galaxies aren't moving into preexisting space, as shrapnel from an exploding bomb would. Instead, space itself is stretching out like perfectly elastic fabric, carrying the galaxies along with it. Second, astronomers believe that no edge exists at all. This doesn't mean the universe is infinitely large; some things, like the surface of a sphere, are finite yet have no edge. Similarly, the cosmos has no boundaries but may not go on forever.

But practically speaking, it might as well. Looking out into space from Earth is similar to looking out at the ocean from a boat: even with the best possible telescope, you can see only so far. You're pretty sure more stuff exists beyond your horizon, but you can't be sure because it's a limit fixed by the geometry of the planet. If you're standing on a small rowboat looking out at the ocean, you can see maybe three miles in any direction, no matter how high-quality a spyglass you use. All of the observable ocean lies within this distance, with very much more beyond.

If you're standing on Earth looking out into space, you can see a little farther, no matter how high-tech your telescope: a little over forty billion light-years in any direction. All of the observable universe, containing hundreds of billions of galaxies, lies within this distance, with very much more beyond.

All That's Really Out There

As our understanding of the universe's size has expanded (and while the universe itself has expanded, faster every day), something else has grown: our knowledge of planets outside the solar system. Within the local arm of our galaxy alone, we've discovered, since 1992, about four thousand planets, called *extrasolar* planets or *exoplanets*, orbiting stars other than the sun. Nearly as many more candidates await confirmation. Multiplying this number up, we estimate that tens of billions of planets exist within the Milky Way alone, not to mention other galaxies. Go outside on a clear night and look up. The overwhelming majority of the stars you see are orbited by planets. Alien worlds are *everywhere*.

It seems likely that at least one of these trillions of planets, somewhere in this practically infinite universe, hosts creatures who think in their own ways, who investigate the cosmos in their own ways, who pray, sing, fight, cry, and write poetry in some alien fashion.

What lies beyond our atom of a planet? What life, what beauty, what violence, what music, what thought, what knowledge, what wisdom, what love? We do not know, and nearly all of us spend our lives not thinking about it. Maybe that's because we, like Tycho, are made uncomfortable by a universe larger and stranger than we expected. We prefer to think that what happens here is the important stuff. But if all of that—voids upon voids and galaxies upon galaxies—is out there, as real as the ground beneath our feet, then maybe we're not so central. If all of that is really out there, then whoever God is may have other things to think about than us. Perhaps it makes us nervous that God so transcends our own powers of comprehension. We presume to know God, but the cosmos suggests that maybe we don't.

Christianity stands as one among many religions found on our humble planet. Our local, particular faith seems mighty provincial in a cosmos such as ours. Maybe a God that large, that strange, that invested in nonhuman worlds, that deep and mysterious, cannot be contained by our one local faith. If this expanding and evolving and practically infinite cosmos is what is next to God, what must God be like? And how in the world can we know?

The Cosmic and the Personal

The biblical book of Job suggests an answer. Rich and wise and healthy and blessed, Job spends his days in his high seat at the city gate, rendering fair judgments and supporting the poor and disenfranchised of his land. Everyone loves him, and why wouldn't they? When someone has a need or a problem, when folks get into arguments, when there's trouble of any sort, Job knows what to do and how to do it. Like a competent and fair father, he takes care of his people.

Like Tycho, Job thought he had a fix on the divine. God, he supposed, was a lot like him: fair, reasonable, and concerned above all with the happiness of human beings. But as he found out the hard way, he was mistaken. Though innocent, he loses his children, his wealth, his health, and his social position all in a very short time. This occurs without warning or explanation. He finds himself on the city ash heap, mourning his losses and angry at God.

Job's greatest wish is for God to show up: "If only I myself, and not another, would behold God with my own eyes," he cries in 19:27. His wish is granted in an unexpected way. Speaking out of a whirlwind, God answers not with an explanation for Job's losses but with a tour of the known universe. God presents Job with creation—the earth, the sky, the stars, the sea. Job gets an eyeful not only of the beautiful and pleasant things but also of the chaotic and violent side of creation. Familiar creatures show up (the wild ass, the ostrich, the lion), but so do monsters such as Behemoth and Leviathan, frightful and alien but, like Job, loved by God. The tour takes Job far from the human world, and God treats him to a perspective from which human civilization appears small and unimportant. The cosmos, untamed and spacious beyond Job's imagination, confounds his expectations.

Unlike Tycho, however, Job gets the point. Realigned to a larger, more mysterious, and more alien universe than he had expected, he is satisfied. "I had heard of you by the hearing of the ear, but now my eye sees you," he says to God in 42:5. Yet Job, like Moses and Isaiah, did not see God; he saw what is *next* to God: an alien and beautiful cosmos, larger than he ever dreamed and filled with curious and uncanny creatures.

This story beautifully balances the cosmic and the personal. Though Job has found himself and all humanity downsized and removed from the center of things, God still shows up in his one tiny particular hour of need. God is not so busy with the ostriches and lions and, for us, the remote galaxies and extraterrestrials that we are abandoned, lost in the cosmos. Job's vision of the universe forces him to expand his understanding of God and even to admit that he does not understand. Our vision of the universe forces us to do the same but does not compel us to lose faith in a God who knows our name, a God who shows up.

Let's try to be less like Tycho and more like Job. Let's not let our idea of God keep us from knowing and loving what God has made, and let's allow the cosmos to help us know God better. Let's not throw away science or faith because the universe is different from what we thought or might even prefer it to be. Let's allow the cosmos to guide us toward an unexpected and mysterious God.

7.

Not Even Wrong: How Science Releases the Bible from Literalism

Anna Bird left on her first interstellar voyage when she was nineteen years old. A few months earlier, her college had awarded her a trip to the Sirius System so she could study the strange bacteria recently discovered there. Excited and a little scared, she hugged her twin brother, Bob, and left Earth for Sirius, 8.6 light-years distant. The year was 2659.

Bob watched as her starship, propelled by a laser-driven light sail, accelerated quickly to near-light speed and disappeared into the shimmer of the Milky Way's Orion-Cygnus arm. He reckoned it would take Anna ten years to reach Sirius, one year to complete her work there, and another ten for her to come back.

As expected, Anna returns twenty-one years later. When she emerges from the ship, Bob, now forty, looks surprised.

"You aged well," he says. "The last twenty-one years have been easy for you."

"What do you mean, twenty-one years?" she replies, smiling. "I've only been gone for eleven. I just turned thirty, old man."

They laugh and embrace. Friends and families always play this game after interstellar trips. Anna really is thirty years old, Bob really is forty, and both of them know it. This time-bending effect of relativity became an everyday fact of life a century before Anna and Bob were born. By

2680, their ten-year age gap seems no more unusual than terraformed planets and thousand-year life spans.

Relativity, Einstein's monumental theory of space and time, tells us (among other things) that time doesn't flow at the same rate for all people at all times. The faster one moves, the slower time crawls, but the effect is too subtle for us to notice in our daily lives. If we routinely zipped around at speeds close to that of light, or if light traveled much slower than it does, this strange flexibility of time would seem commonplace to us today, just as it does for Anna and Bob in 2680.

The Brain-Teaser Bible

Here in the twenty-first century, some people look at this time-stretching weirdness of relativity and see possibilities for science fiction—*The Sparrow, Interstellar, Arrival,* and *Contact* are just a few books and films that rely on this very real effect, called *time dilation*. Others see scientific and technological benefits, from particle physics to cosmology to GPS. Still others take a philosophical approach, claiming (incorrectly) that Einstein's theory teaches that all points of view, no matter how different they might seem, are equally valid.[1]

But perhaps the most novel use of relativity has been proposed by physicist and author Gerald Schroeder, who uses Einstein's theory to reconcile science and the Bible. Science, with its 13.8 billion years of cosmic and biological evolution, presents a stiff challenge to those who consider the six days of creation in Genesis 1 to be actual twenty-four-hour days. Wishing to hold onto the literal meaning of both timelines, Schroeder uses time dilation to show that a set of events that lasts 13.8 billion years in one frame of reference might last only six days in another, thereby reconciling a plain reading of Genesis 1 with modern science.[2]

It's possible to look at the Bible this way, but that doesn't mean it's a good idea. Schroeder's attempt at reconciliation through relativity reminds me of a remark once made by Wolfgang Pauli, one of the architects of quantum mechanics. Late in Pauli's career, a colleague brought him a paper written by a young physicist who hoped to hear what the great scientist thought of it. After taking a look, he handed it back to his colleague and said sadly, "It is not even wrong."[3]

Sometimes an answer to a question comes from a perspective so removed from and so out of touch with the question itself that it cannot even be said to be wrong. Imagine asking someone the meaning of life, the universe, and everything, and their answer comes back, "Forty-two." Or imagine asking someone how far it is to the next gas station, and they reply, "The Battle of Hastings." Such responses do not even rise to the level of being wrong.

Schroeder makes a similar mistake when he applies the intricacies of twentieth-century theoretical physics to an ancient religious text. Genesis emerged out of a particular cultural context and was written for a particular theological purpose. It concerns itself with the meaning of human life and with the various relationships between God, humanity, and creation. It tells us who we are and who God is. It aligns us with the deepest truths about ourselves—our creativity, our joys, our hopes, our fears, our capacities for great love and great evil—and it accounts for the beauty and rationality of creation. It does all of this using the primary mediums of its age: prose and poetry, not the abstractions of contemporary mathematical physics.

I wonder how Schroeder understands the Bible. I wonder what he thinks it is. It's hard to imagine applying relativity to Genesis without thinking of the Bible as some kind of secret code to be cracked. But this view is alien to the source and spirit and intent of Scripture. It is not even wrong. It shrinks the Bible down to the size of a riddle or puzzle or other such amusement. Scripture is not a brain teaser. No Easter eggs have been buried there, waiting to be discovered by Einstein's, or anyone else's, science.

Taking the Temperature of the Universe

So Genesis concerns itself with God and relationships. But this doesn't mean it can't be about science, too, right? Maybe it does faith *and* science, much as Ruthie Ann Wright does chess *and* boxing.

Let's find out. Take your Bible and count back the years from the time of Jesus, and you'll find that creation week occurred about six thousand years ago.[4] Many people, like the creationists we met earlier, believe this to be an accurate date for the origin of the universe and that creation occurred in six twenty-four-hour days, as a plain reading of Genesis indicates. But this conclusion works only so long as you reject the mountain of scientific evidence standing against it.

Suppose a child wakes up one morning, feeling bad. Her dad places his hand on her forehead and says, "You're hot." He breaks out the in-ear thermometer, and it reports 102.2 degrees. Just to be sure, he digs around in the back of the medicine cabinet and pulls out the old mercury thermometer. After two minutes, it reads 102.0. Does the little girl have a fever? Yes. Three independent measurements say so.

To be sure, the methods are not equally reliable, and the numbers vary somewhat, but her temperature is definitely in the neighborhood of 102. It might be 101.9 and it might be 102.3, but it doesn't matter, because Dad knows what he needs to know: it's time to call the doctor.

As he picks up the phone, a crazy thought occurs to him: maybe she faked it. Maybe, immediately before complaining about feeling bad, she placed a heating pad to her forehead, tweaked the electronics of the in-ear device so it would read several degrees high, rooted around for the old mercury thermometer, and held it up to a hot lamp for a few minutes before returning it to its place in the rear of the cabinet. But he swiftly recognizes this scenario as impossibly convoluted and out of character for his little girl. He smiles to himself, sets his aberrant thought aside, and calls the pediatrician.

Scientists have concluded that the universe is about 13.8 billion years old. Like the 102-degree fever, this figure is drawn from several different kinds of measurements. Three of these are (1) observations of a class of stars called *white dwarfs*, (2) details of something called the *cosmic microwave background*, and (3) the recession velocities of distant galaxies. These methods all point to an age in the neighborhood of 13.8 billion years. If the true age of the universe differs significantly from this value, then these methods—and others I've not mentioned—must not only be wrong individually but also be wrong *in the same way* so they all give the same result. But as in the case of the sick child, these observations do not overlap and do not depend on the same assumptions, so the probability of them all giving the same wrong answer really is zero (unless, as with the sick girl, a good deal of convoluted and before-the-fact system rigging has taken place).

Just as in the measurement of the child's temperature, different methods give us slightly different ages. The universe might be 13.7 billion years old according to the microwave background and 13.9 billion according to galactic recession, but we know what we need to know: the cosmos is many billions of years old, far older than a plain reading of the Bible allows.

A different (and larger) group of observations don't pin the age of the cosmos at 13.8 billion years but do tell us it is far older than six thousand years. Three of these observations are (1) measurements of the distances of nearby stars, (2) surveys of radioactive nuclei found in Earth's crust, and (3) the drifting of continental plates. Again, these methods *independently* point to the same conclusion: Earth and the cosmos have been around *much* longer than six thousand years.

Climbing the Distance Ladder

If the universe weren't so old, it couldn't be so big. It has been expanding ever since the big bang, and by now it spans many billions of light-years. Astronomers deploy a whole series of overlapping methods for determining distances to stars and galaxies, and these procedures work together to form something called the *distance ladder*.

Distances to the closest stars are measured by parallax, the method used by Thomas Henderson to nail down the position of Alpha Centauri.[5] More distant objects require other methods. Some of these methods provide more reliable values than others, but steady progress and cross-checking cause the distance ladder to tighten up and give better and better results over time. This progress has been made through advances in telescope technology and refinements of observing methods.

Parallax and other low rungs of the distance ladder don't provide much perspective, but the high rungs demonstrate the great age of the universe. If we can see galaxies millions and even billions of light-years away, that means the cosmos must have been around for millions and even billions of years. If it wasn't, the light from these distant galaxies could never have reached us.

Important assumptions lie beneath all of this. For example, we assume that the speed of light is constant; that is, it was the same a billion years ago as it is today. We also assume that rates of radioactivity have not changed over time and that the physics that applies way out there is the same as the physics that applies here on Earth. Scientists are keenly aware of these and other assumptions and test them constantly. So far, the assumptions have stood all tests.

One hundred percent certainty is not possible in science, but one good reason to trust our assumptions is that they have led us to a self-consistent understanding of the cosmos. For a simple example of this, the age of Earth is less than the age of the universe, even though the ages of both are determined in completely different ways. Also, the age of the universe is greater but not much greater than the age of the oldest stars. And the time required for stars to produce the elements needed for life is *far* less than the age of the universe. The list goes on.

To be sure, some pieces of the puzzle don't fit. Major questions are still being asked (for example, what is causing cosmic expansion to accelerate?). This is to be expected; it has always been so. But the scientific work of the last five centuries gives a clear sense of increasing consistency and fruitfulness. This would be quite surprising if our assumptions were all wrong.

God the Con Artist

Only one argument remains available to anyone who wishes to hold onto a literal understanding of Genesis. Like the little girl working ahead of time, contriving a false measurement of her temperature, God could have carefully constructed the cosmos to appear to be much older than it is. Perhaps God rigged it to look billions of light-years across. Maybe light from "distant" stars and galaxies was created in midflight; maybe South America and Africa, including minute details of their geology and biology, were formed to look exactly as if they were part of a single, original continent and have been drifting apart for two hundred million years; maybe the cosmic microwave background radiation, a relic of the big bang, was put in place to make the cosmos seem billions of years old.

But why would God deliberately tweak the cosmos to appear—in every detail and from every scientific angle—not just old but precisely 13.8 billion years old? To test our reliance on the literal words of the Bible?

That's not even wrong. Any God that would manipulate the universe in such a way—just to examine human beings with a senseless test of our dedication not to God but to a particular and strained interpretation of the Bible— cannot be trusted. That anti-rational agent of disorder would not deserve our devotion and trust. That God roots for us to reject our own God-given capacities for reason, imagination, and creativity. That God bears no resemblance to the Lord of life and love and reason and wonder to whom the Bible ultimately points. That God contradicts Scripture in ways that *really* matter.

In 1615, Galileo wrote, "I do not feel obliged to believe that the same God who has endowed us with sense, reason, and intellect has intended us to forgo their use."[6] With him, I hope, we can all agree.

8.

A Scientist Reads the Bible: How Science Enlarges Scripture

"The world, I believe, is honestly flat."[1]

Thus did "Mad" Mike Hughes, a California limousine driver, explain why he launched himself 1,875 feet above the Mojave Desert in his homemade steam-powered rocket. The feat, performed on March 24, 2018, took him a step closer to his ultimate goal of rising so high that he sees—or doesn't see—the curvature of Earth with his own eyes. Alas for Hughes: commercial aircraft, flying at more than twenty times his maximum altitude, do not go high enough for passengers to detect Earth's curve. Only military pilots and astronauts reach the required altitudes of more than fifty thousand feet.

Hughes has company in his suspicion of "ballers," as round-Earth proponents are sometimes called. The number of flat-Earthers has ticked upward over the last several years. Certain celebrities (including rapper B.o.B) are certified, while others have come out as "flat-curious." According to the *Denver Post*, flat-Earth groups have begun meeting in coffee bars and private homes in Denver, Boston, New York, Houston, Philadelphia, Phoenix, and Chicago.[2] The second annual Flat Earth International Conference took place in Denver in November 2018 and the third is planned for Dallas in late 2019.

I cannot adequately express my dismay at this trend.

Unlike many ideas in science, the round-Earth theory is easily proved. You don't even need to launch yourself into space to do it. Just take a pair of binoculars to any large body of water and watch a boat sail away from shore. Through the binoculars, you'll see the ship disappear hull first.[3] The highest part of the ship will be seen last. And this will happen no matter which direction it sails. In no case will the boat simply shrink and disappear into a point, as it would on a flat ocean.

Aristotle was the first to provide a full scientific argument in favor of a spherical Earth. His claim is based on three independent observations: one from the sailing ship and two from astronomy. He composed this argument hundreds of years before Jesus was born, and it still stands as a beautifully articulated and easily understood scientific theory.

The (Biblical) Earth Is Flat

Hughes, B.o.B, and other flat-Earthers have managed to ignore twenty-four centuries of the most basic science. But in their view of the universe, they have esteemed company: the authors of Genesis 1. The first book of the Bible describes the cosmos as envisioned by ancient Israel, a cosmos centered on a very flat Earth.

Shortly after the breath of God moves across the waters and the first light explodes into existence, a dome, or firmament, separates the "waters from the waters." God calls this dome *sky* before dry land emerges from the waters below the dome. Then plants, sun and moon and stars, fish, birds, animals, and people are added to the scene. Further along in Scripture, pillars of the heavens and Earth are thrown in, and the underworld, too. The whole thing looks like a hemispherical bubble floating in a universe of water.

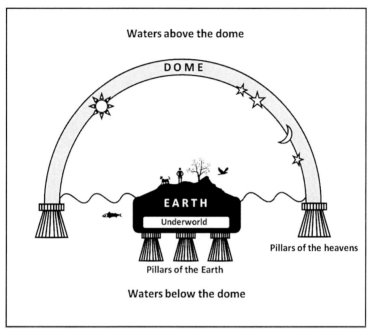

The cosmos according to Genesis 1.

The differences between this cosmos and ours, with its black holes, colossal voids, quasars, galactic cannibalism, neutron stars, dark energy, virtual particles, gravitational waves, dwarf planets, near-Earth asteroids, fusion-powered stars, elastic space-time, cosmic microwave background radiation, and billions of years of gradually evolving and interrelated life, cannot be overstated. If the Bible were intended to be a science book, we'd have thrown it out centuries ago.

But this makes it hard to see why science matters at all when we read the Bible, and in a certain very narrow sense, it *doesn't* matter. No matter what theory scientists come up with, if God ever loved us, God will love us still; if Jesus ever mattered, he will matter still; and if justice and reconciliation were ever our calling, they will be our calling still. It seems that the shape of the universe has nothing to do with our daily human experience of God and one another.

Motion, Lit by Fusion

But we live in a scientific age. We read our Bibles not on a flat Earth under a transparent dome but on a spherical planet orbiting a star revolving about the center of a vast galactic pinwheel, turning among black holes and quasars. *These* are the things God has made.

We cannot set aside what we know and what we love when we sit down with Scripture, nor are we asked to. Jesus commands us to love God with all our *mind* as well as with our heart, soul, and strength. There is such a thing as the scientific love of God. Those who wish to take both faith and science seriously must hold the Bible in one hand and *Scientific American* in the other.

Science, in its proper context, deepens and enlarges everything it touches. The night sky supplies a perfect example. Its beauty is available to all. But an astronomer looking at the sky sees that beauty and more. She sees the moon in the east and imagines its gradual outward spiral. She sees a string of planets—Saturn, Mars, Venus, Mercury —like a diamond necklace running downward toward the western horizon. She knows Jupiter, Uranus, and Neptune turn under her feet. She gains a palpable sense of Earth's place and motion through the tilted, turning solar system. These things sit in the foreground like bugs on a windshield compared with the stars beyond and the long arc of the circling galaxy, and she sees it all at once. She spots the Andromeda Galaxy in the southwest and can almost feel it falling, ninety miles per second, toward her. Beyond that, she can imagine vast voids and walls of galaxies, galaxy clusters, and quasars stretching outward to an infinite horizon. It's all in motion and lit by fusion, and every piece of this panorama evokes wonder and teases her with new questions.

Let the Waters Bring Forth Swarms of Euthycarcinoids

Something similar happens when a biblical scholar reads the Bible. Like the stars on a clear night, the words sit there on the page, freely available to all. But depth beyond depth is revealed to those who have read it closely for years, learned the original languages, studied the history and culture of the ancient Near East, and become acquainted with biblical theology and the history of biblical interpretation. The more you know, the more you see, and the more questions occur to you.

Now, what happens when a *scientist* reads the Bible? It depends on the scientist. Some dismiss it outright, for Scripture has little to say about science as we know it today. But for me, a scientist who has not rejected the Bible, a fascinating new set of connections opens up, connections not available to nonscientists. When I read Scripture, I draw on three resources. First, I have the words on the page, as everyone else does. Second, I have my own set of personal, cultural, theological, linguistic, and interpretive meanings I picked up at church, in Sunday school, at home, during my years at a religious high school, and at seminary. Third, I have a lively host of scientific extras.

These extras are not essential to my core understanding of the Bible. They are bonuses, supplements, new and fun ideas neither demanded nor contradicted by my basic view of Scripture as a human record of Israel's encounter with a real and loving God. Why even mention these extras, then, if they are secondary? I see three reasons: (1) science *does* describe the creation of Israel's real and loving God; (2) I think of these bonuses every time I read the Bible, and I can't stop thinking of them; and (3) our approach to the Bible should be as free and creative and imaginative as the God who inspired it.

Consider an example from Genesis 1:

> And God said, "Let the waters bring forth swarms of living creatures, and let birds fly above the earth across the dome of the sky." So God created the great sea monsters and every living creature that moves, of every kind, with which the waters swarm, and every winged bird of every kind. . . .

> And God said, "Let the earth bring forth living creatures of every kind: cattle and creeping things and wild animals of the earth of every kind." And it was so. God made the wild animals of the earth of every kind, and the cattle of every kind, and everything that creeps upon the ground of every kind. (Genesis 1:20–21, 24–25)

Notice this: "the waters" and "the earth" bring forth living creatures. These verses suggest that God creates indirectly, using what was previously made. God's creation creates!

This passage invites us to imagine evolution in all its weirdness and beauty. We are free to visualize life being brought forth deep in the waters, perhaps microorganisms thriving on hydrothermal vents on the ocean floor four billion years ago. We may envision euthycarcinoids, distant ancestors of centipedes who left the sea 530 million years ago, beating even plants in life's slow landward creep. The Middle Cambrian oddball *Opabinia* provides a colorful side note. This five-eyed, backward-mouthed, limbless, long-nosed, sea-dwelling anthropod was one of the first and strangest animals to ever live.

The authors of Genesis, whoever they were, knew nothing of evolution or hydrothermal vents or euthycarcinoids or *Opabinia*. God did not whisper these verses into their ears, knowing we would eventually figure out evolution and discover the secret truth of Scripture. Instead, they observed nature, saw that God had given it the capacity to generate new things, and wove this insight into their creation story.

The Monsters Arrived on Boxing Day

Another scientific bonus appears in the reading of the Old Testament book of Job. Near the end of the book, God praises a great and terrible pair of beasts: Behemoth, monster of the land, and Leviathan, monster of the sea:

> Look at Behemoth,
>   which I made just as I made [Job];
>   it eats grass like an ox.
> Its strength is in its loins,
>   and its power in the muscles of its belly.
> It makes its tail stiff like a cedar;
>   the sinews of its thighs are knit together.
> Its bones are tubes of bronze,
>   its limbs like bars of iron.
> It is the first of the great acts of God—
>   only its Maker can approach it with the sword.
> (Job 40:15–19)

> Its [Leviathan's] heart is as hard as stone,
>   as hard as the lower millstone.
> When it raises itself up the gods are afraid;
>   at the crashing they are beside themselves.

Though the sword reaches it, it does not avail,
  nor does the spear, the dart, or the javelin.
It counts iron as straw,
  and bronze as rotten wood.
The arrow cannot make it flee;
  slingstones, for it, are turned to chaff.
. . . .
On earth it has no equal,
  a creature without fear. (Job 41:24–29, 33)

The ancient Israelites were aware of the dangers of creation. They knew of the great powers of earth and storm and surf, the chaotic forces of the cosmos. Behemoth and Leviathan represent these destructive powers in the stories and poetry of the Bible, including these verses. It therefore seems strange that God should heap praise and admiration on them. What good could possibly come of such de-creative forces?

A little knowledge of science brings this strangeness into focus and drives us to ask some interesting theological questions. If you take a hard-boiled egg, hold it a foot or so over your kitchen counter, and drop it, the shell will shatter but stay stuck to the egg. Earth is like this: its crust (three to thirty miles thick) covers the planet but is crisscrossed by deep cracks. About a dozen large pieces, or *plates,* make up the whole crust. But, unlike our pieces of eggshell, these plates do not stay still. They move relative to each other at speeds of an inch or two per year. This may not seem like much, but it's only an average, and the plates do not progress smoothly. A hundred years of stillness can be followed by a few seconds of monstrous violence.

On December 26, 2004, at 00:59 Universal Time,[4] the Indian plate (which carries the Indian Ocean as well as India itself) slid about fifty feet under the Burma plate (which carries a small collection of islands off the coast of Myanmar), pushing it suddenly upward. This took several minutes and resulted in one of the most severe earthquakes on record. The violent shifting of the ocean floor caused a tsunami, which crashed ashore in various countries, destroying cities, causing billions of dollars in damage, and taking nearly 230,000 human lives.[5] Some died as far away as South Africa.

Now, if you've ever struggled to understand what irony is, consider this example: the very process that took so many lives—plate tectonics—is necessary for life to exist and thrive on Earth in the first place.[6] This suggests that God created and admires Behemoth and Leviathan because those powers of chaos are *necessary*. Perhaps these same powers are channeled by God into the very good creation of living things. It may sound strange to place limits on divine power, but perhaps even God can't create life in a perfectly safe cosmos.

Now, I don't know if this is true or not, and I don't think earth science holds the secret key to Scripture, but we are always free to ask such questions and to follow where they lead. God can certainly handle it.

Riding a Rocket to Hell

When I read the prophet Isaiah, I think of Elon Musk, the greatest American inventor and innovator of our time, and the planet Mars.

On May 12, 2018, Musk tweeted, "The goal of BFR is to enable anyone to move to the moon, Mars, & eventually outer planets." The Big Falcon Rocket, or BFR, which is being developed by Musk and his space company SpaceX, will bring Musk one step closer to his dream of colonizing the solar system.

It won't come easily. Mars alone presents stiff challenges. It is hell on Mars for our bodies. Gravity on the Red Planet is much feebler than here at home, so after we spend some time on Mars, our bones and muscles will grow weak (and this process may not be reversible). The average temperature on Mars runs near –67°F, so we couldn't play baseball, sunbathe, or do walkathons. The atmosphere is composed almost entirely of carbon dioxide and contains only a trace of oxygen. There's no way we could breathe it. The thin atmosphere allows lots of ultraviolet light to reach the surface, so cancer, cognitive disease, and reproductive problems will multiply. The planet lacks a magnetic field, so it's constantly bombarded by fast-moving electrons and protons from the sun. Even more cancer. Mars orbits farther from the sun than Earth, so even bright days would seem dim. This fact, combined with the lack of surface water and organics in the soil, makes it impossible to grow food—or anything else, for that matter. Also, no germs live on Mars, so our immune systems will lose their ability to fight any diseases that may arrive on spaceships from Earth.

This makes our home planet seem so much more, well, homey. Surely we belong among the rivers and trees of Earth. Isaiah makes this plain:

> For thus says the Lord,
> who created the heavens
>   (he is God!),
> who formed the earth and made it
>   (he established it;
> he did not create it a chaos,
>   he formed it to be inhabited!). (Isaiah 45:18)

> I will open rivers on the bare heights,
>   and fountains in the midst of the valleys;
> I will make the wilderness a pool of water,

and the dry land springs of water.
I will put in the wilderness the cedar,
   the acacia, the myrtle, and the olive;
I will set in the desert the cypress,
   the plane and the pine together,
so that all may see and know,
   all may consider and understand,
that the hand of the Lord has done this,
   the Holy One of Israel has created it. (Isaiah 41:18–20)

What a contrast to the lifeless, desolate, radiation-saturated, frozen, dry, alien, hellish world of Mars.

But scientifically speaking, our fit with Earth is no more surprising than a puddle's fit with a sidewalk. We belong on Earth because we were drawn out of it and have evolved along with it. Evolution's great stream carries us and the rest of the planet along together.

And if we were ever to leap the high hurdles I mentioned (and more) and successfully colonize Mars, the same could one day be said of us and that planet. We could evolve to fit there as snugly as we do here. The Martians would eventually come to feel very much at home on the Red Planet. (We would probably want to keep Earthlings and Martians mixed, however. If we don't, the two groups will, after many generations, evolve into separate species, just as a single species divides into two when separated on Earth.)

So, when I read these passages from Isaiah, this thought comes to me as a bonus: God has not made us specially to fit into a static, preexisting world as a piece fits into a jig-saw puzzle. Instead, God has created and is still creating us along with a universe in which we might ever find a home here, on Mars, and maybe one day beyond the solar system.

Free to Imagine

You may disagree with what I am doing here. You may think that it's wrongheaded to drag evolution into a discussion of Genesis because that book is really about relationships between God, humanity, and creation. Some will laugh at my application of geology to the book of Job, because the questions of death and suffering are not meaningfully addressed by plate tectonics. And knowledgeable critics will point out that Isaiah's poetry is meant not to show how nicely we fit into the biosphere but to contrast Israel's good, green future with the lifeless desolation of the Babylonian exile.

But I do not intend to replace standard understandings of Scripture with scientific ones. These examples show how science deepens, sharpens, or expands traditional meanings. Christians who love science are free to imagine new things when they come to Scripture, to create a kind of scientific commentary on the Bible. These examples show how Scripture might be enlarged, and not reduced or replaced, by science.

9.

The Things God Has Made: How Science Enlarges Our View of Life and Death

As a writer and speaker, I receive a lot of questions. Some people want to know how I reconcile creation and evolution. Others ask about miracles, or what I think about the star of Bethlehem, or how Jesus fits into evolution. But some of my favorites come from fans of popular science who ask about far-out stuff like string theory, going faster than light, wormholes, the multiverse, extra dimensions, time travel, whether or not the universe is a hologram, and so forth.

Last year, I spoke to a congregation in St. Louis. The presentation featured a timeline that stretched from the big bang to the present moment and included both cosmic and biological evolution. After the talk, I opened the floor for questions. A woman in the front row raised her hand. "I enjoyed your presentation," she said and then worked her away around to one of the more popular of these far-out but fair questions: "What happened before the big bang?"

Usually when people ask this, they're picturing *something* existing before all the stars and galaxies showed up, even if it's just empty space waiting around for the great boom. So I explain that empty space is not a thing. Even space containing zero normal matter and set to a temperature of absolute zero—a condition known as the *quantum vacuum*—simmers with short-lived electromagnetic fields and particle-antiparticle pairs popping into and out of existence.

Nevertheless, she asked a fine question. And the answer is that no one knows what happened before the big bang. Some say nothing at all happened because there was no space or time for anything to happen in, that both space and time were produced by the cosmic kaboom, along with light and electrons and galaxies and coral and frogs and you and me.

Others believe that something must have existed before $t = 0$, but we probably can't know the answer. The conditions at the time of the bang prevent us from knowing what, if anything, happened before it. The big bang stands like a wall in time, and there's no seeing through it or around it. So I usually tell my audience that, as sensible as the question sounds, asking what happened before the big bang is a little like asking what's south of the South Pole. The question is out of bounds by definition.

Saint Augustine, one of the chief architects of Christian theology, might nod in agreement. To the question "What was God doing before he made heaven and earth?" Augustine preferred the reply "I do not know what I do not know," though he seemed to favor the nothing-at-all option.[1]

Which brings me to my point. The woman's question, I suspect, was not prompted by simple scientific curiosity. Theology often lurks in the background of such questions, especially when asked inside a church. Behind her question I heard, "Yes, all this evolution business is fine, but it's really God that wound it all up and let it rip, right?" She wanted to make sure I haven't pushed God out of the picture, that there's a place for the Creator in an evolving cosmos.

No one can blame her for wanting to make sure of this, but a faulty assumption is at work here, a fallacy called the *God of the gaps*. It says God acts in those places science can't reach, such as before the big bang. But the history of science shows that, time after time, science has advanced into quarters previously thought beyond its scope.

For centuries, the heavens were considered to be unreachable by science. No one knew why the planets never stopped moving, so they chalked it up to divine agents: God's wisdom, or intelligences, or angels kept them going. But in the late seventeenth century, Isaac Newton worked it all out in a spectacular theory called gravity. He wasn't vague about it either; he was mathematically precise, and he was right.[2] His theory described the motion not only of the planets but of the moon, and of comets, and of apples falling from trees, *in detail*. There was no fuzz on Newton's solutions. With astounding accuracy and precision, he predicted that Earth bulges at its equator and that the sun wobbles in a fantastically complex pattern as the planets move around it. And, thanks to the surprising motion of Uranus, he predicted that the planet Neptune exists. Newton's fabulous success suggested that God's wisdom or angels didn't keep the moon in motion; gravity did. So God was shuffled off to a place science hadn't yet reached: biology (Newton predated Darwin by nearly two centuries). This kind of thinking results in God shrinking, because it means that whenever science advances, God retreats. As the scientifically uncharted reaches of the universe diminish, so does God. This has been going on for hundreds of years, and today God has been squeezed into dark corners such as the human brain, a weird phenomenon known as *quantum uncertainty*, something called *chaos*, and whatever was happening before the big bang.

But God belongs in the light as well as the dark. We must release God (really, our *idea* of God) from such cramped quarters. We must allow our ideas about the Creator to be as free and imaginative as the Creator. Yes, God is a mystery, and we see through a glass darkly, but it is central to Christianity that God is revealed in what is seen and known. "The heavens are telling of the glory of God," writes the psalmist. "Day to day [they] pour forth speech, and night to night declare knowledge" (19:1a, 2). Paul writes in the book of Romans that "ever since the creation of the world [God's] eternal power and divine nature, invisible though they are, have been understood and seen through the things God has made" (1:20).

Very well. Let us turn and look, then, at the things God has made.

From the Big Bang to Bieber

God said, "Let there be light," and there was light.

As we saw earlier, you shouldn't try to match up the Genesis 1 timeline with events in scientifically approved cosmic history. Nevertheless, this is an uncanny way for God to start things off, for it seems that light, and lots of it, really was the first product of the big bang.

It's a mighty long road from pure light to modern human civilization. From the light must come both matter and antimatter, but not in precisely equal amounts. For every 1,000,000,000 antiparticles, you need 1,000,000,001 particles. Then these excess particles—hydrogen and a little helium, mostly—must be formed into stars. Then you need to wait around for several billion years while heavier elements—carbon and oxygen and magnesium and iron and so forth—are cooked inside stars and dying stars and supernovas. These nuclei must be bound together just right—not too loose, not too tight—and then they need to collect some stray electrons and drift around the cosmos for a few hundred million years or more, settle down on a nice planet—not too hot, not too cold—and assemble themselves into molecules, then bigger molecules, then (somehow) something like bacteria, which must, a billion years later, evolve into algae, then fish and amphibians and reptiles and strange ratlike primates and hominids, and finally, *Homo sapiens*. Somewhere along the line, consciousness must get folded in. Only then can we get stone tools and controlled fire and domesticated animals and the wheel and pyramids and chariots and nation-states and Justin Bieber.

(And please remember: the bacteria and fish and amphibians and reptiles and primates became more than us. They became *Streptococcus* and swordfish and rattlesnakes and magpies and silverback gorillas and on and on. They and other prehistoric oddities fanned out into the millions of species that now cover the planet, from ghostfish five miles below the surface of the ocean to Rüppell's vultures flying at altitudes of thirty-seven thousand feet, from Somali wild asses living through 120-degree Ethiopian summers to arctic ground squirrels who survive by supercooling their bodies to 27 degrees Fahrenheit—well below freezing—seven months a year.)

It took 13.8 billion years to get from the big bang to Justin Bieber. To get a sense of what this means, imagine compressing this time span into a single calendar year. The big bang happened on New Year's Day, and we, along with JB, are at this moment ringing out the year at midnight on December 31. On this time scale, the last forty-five centuries—the time since the building of the great pyramids—have come and gone in the time it took you to read this sentence.

This long unfurling of light, matter, and life could not have happened if a separate set of unlikely things had not been true. For example, if the universe did not contain three dimensions of space and one of time, or if the cosmic mass-energy density were not balanced on a knife edge called $\Omega = 1$, or if the rate at which stars fuse hydrogen into helium were not precisely as it is, or if the relative strengths of the electromagnetic and gravitational forces did not equal approximately 1,000,000,000,000,000,000, 000,000,000,000,000,000, we could not be here to talk about it. There are more requirements, but these are sufficient to make my point: the world is a miracle, as are we in it.

Riding the Red Wave

But the story is not all starlight and fine, sturdy creatures. If you turn the coin of evolution bright side down and consider its opposite face, you'll encounter a nasty, brutish affair that runs on chance and death. You'll see that *Homo sapiens* is riding the leading edge of a great red tsunami, a four-billion-year tidal wave of violence and suffering.

Species don't survive. They arrive to vanish, just as individuals do, and every hundred million years or so, the tsunami surges, and a worldwide mass extinction swallows large numbers of species in a short amount of time.[3] Once the waves pass, new species rapidly emerge in a global game of chomp-or-be-chomped in which death spurs evolution to do its best and most creative work. But it is not pretty work. During these periods of great diversification, evolution dreams up a million ideas a minute and throws them all against the wall. Only a few stick. Death is the rule; survival is the exception.

This horrible inefficiency rules individual lives also. For some species, a great many creatures must be born for a single one to survive to maturity. This doesn't hold for human beings, but it probably used to. It remains true for many creatures, especially certain small ones, for which the odds against any given individual's survival to adulthood are millions, even billions, to one.

Consider the wildly experimental, trial-and-error, failure-stricken, blood-soaked lives of such disregarded creatures as horsehair worms, blood flukes, and gooseneck barnacles. These beings are ordained to live out their lives within single-elimination obstacle courses that make *American Ninja Warrior* look like a walk to the mailbox. Billions of barnacle larvae fail to clear the hoops, scale the walls, and stick the landings for every one that successfully reaches full adult barnaclehood. So many tiny, silent deaths leave us wondering, "What kind of God are we dealing with here?"

Certain scorpions, spiders, and crabs engage in *matriphagy*, or the eating of a mother by her offspring. Insects galore die when they are devoured from the inside out by wasp or worm larvae previously deposited by another creature or inadvertently swallowed. Some species, even big mammals like chimpanzees, sloth bears, and lions, are known to eat their young without warning and without known cause.

These, too, are the things God has made. "God's eternal power and divine nature" has apparently been expressed by billions of years of inefficiency, arbitrary suffering, and violence. God may have opted for the long road, but it's a hard and bloody one, too.

Two Thoughts

I don't know why the universe returns such a mixed verdict—equal and inseparable parts life and death, health and suffering, but I have two thoughts about it.

First, I'd like to point out how shocking it is that we find ourselves within a universe in the first place and are able to bear witness to it, know it, form sentences about it, and communicate about these things we call life and death. We often fail to appreciate and honor the simple fact of existence. Children are endlessly fascinated by sparrows, click pens, rain, hands, ants, the moon, cracks in the sidewalk, dirt, coins, the shapes of leaves, wind, and every other feature of reality, no matter how inconsequential. The sources of childhood wonder go on for pages, books, libraries. Having been so recently and startlingly dropped into being, they live in a state of perpetual wonder.

This experience fades as we grow up. This is as it should be, to an extent, because we can't spend our afternoons collecting beetles in the backyard when we have bills to pay. But we should periodically be reminded of the gratuitous and astonishing gift of existence. Art and stories and poetry and music and science and walks in the woods and acts of love large and small have the power to draw us back into wonder, the fountainhead of both faith and science.

When we lose our capacity for wonder, we dishonor existence and forfeit the ability to place death and suffering in their proper context. The thought of that great red tsunami will overwhelm us only if we fail to back up, take a larger view, and see all life as a gift. I do not mean to downplay death or minimize suffering but to suggest wonder, which I think of as a pointed awareness of and gratitude for the gift of existence, as an antidote to their poison.

Second, the Creator has not abandoned us on this beautiful but bloody planet. God knows firsthand the worst our violent universe can dish out. God weeps, God suffers, God dies, and God lives. Jesus's birth, life, death, and resurrection reveal a truth of the universe as fundamental as relativity and quantum mechanics, so often lost in Jesus-died-for-you billboards and bumper stickers and hackneyed religious formulas: through vulnerable, self-giving love, there is hope not only for *Homo sapiens* but for all creation—for lions, scorpions, horsehair worms, and even for those poor gooseneck barnacles.

Jesus, no less than you and me and *T. rex,* was born into the flow of evolution and is therefore intimately bound up not only with human beings but with every single creature that has ever lived and will ever live, no matter how strange or insignificant.[4] He is connected to creation *as a whole* and every single thing in it, literally and with no exceptions. This is because biological evolution is a small part of a much larger and older cosmic evolution that got started long before life showed up on Earth.

When we accept evolution, we see that God is woven into the very fabric of all material reality, not just the human or even the conscious part of it. In taking on the violence and suffering inherent in physical reality, Jesus transformed it, revealing the great love of God for all creatures and all things everywhere, here and throughout the cosmos.

10.

At Home with Miracle Max: How Science Expands Our Understanding of Miracles

Inigo and Fezzik have a lot to do. They must storm Prince Humperdinck's castle, stop his wedding, kill the evil Count Rugen, and rescue Princess Buttercup, and they need to do it *now*. But they can't do any of it without the Man in Black.

Trouble is, the Man in Black is dead. So Inigo and Fezzik have brought his body to Miracle Max, hoping the crabby old wonder-worker will bring it back to life. The body is laid out flat on Max's kitchen table. Max stands before it, poking it, muttering to himself, lost in thought, taking his time.

"Sir," says Inigo softly.[1]

"What?"

"We're in a terrible rush."

Max looks up. "You got money?"

"Sixty-five," says Inigo.

"Sheesh! I never worked for so little. OK, so what does he have here that's worth living for?" he asks.

Trying to keep their plans hidden, Inigo makes up a story. Max doesn't buy it.

"Aren't you a rotten liar," he says, shaking his head. He

looks back down at the Man in Black and says, "He probably owes you money. Well, I'll ask him."

"He's dead; he can't talk," says a befuddled Inigo.

"Oooh, look who knows so much!" Max says. "Well, it just so happens that your friend here is only *mostly* dead. There's a big difference between *mostly* dead and *all* dead. *Mostly dead* is *slightly alive*. Now, *all dead*—with *all dead*, there is usually only one thing you can do."

"What's that?" asks Inigo.

"Go through his clothes and look for loose change."

Max makes the miracle pill, mostly-dead becomes all-alive, the castle is stormed, Humperdinck's wedding is stopped, Inigo prevails over Count Rugen, the Man in Black marries the princess, and with the notable exceptions of Humperdinck and Rugen, everyone lives happily ever after.

One Miracle, Two Worlds

This scene, from the hugely entertaining movie *The Princess Bride*, has something to teach us about miracles, something that may challenge the common understanding of the word. Normally, people think of a miracle as a surprising and happy event that cannot be explained by science and is therefore considered to be the work of some divine agent. In other words, the world normally operates by natural laws, and a miracle is what happens when God breaks or suspends those laws in order to help us out.

On June 7, 2014, Grayson Kirby was thrown from a vehicle and was thought to be dead upon arrival at the hospital. His lungs were punctured and crushed, his ribs were broken along with many other bones in his body, and his kidneys were damaged.

Machines stabilized his heart, and a ventilator provided oxygen, but he was in a coma for ten days, and his vital signs dropped to zero twice during that time. Doctors gave him a 5 percent chance of survival. But they told his family his brain had suffered great trauma and that, even if he did survive, he would never be the same.

But Kirby made a full recovery. His brain functions perfectly, and he has returned to complete health. According to him, his personality has actually improved. His doctors could not explain it, but his family and friends could.

It was "lots of prayers," said Michelle Ciucci, a family friend. "His Facebook page had like 8,600 followers, and they all prayed hard for him."[2] On his TV show, Steve Harvey said to Grayson's mother, "You called his survival a miracle. Why?"

"The doctors could give us no hope. . . . But, you know, the power of prayer is amazing." At this the audience erupted in applause. "We had nine thousand people all around the world praying," she said.

Steve turned to Grayson and asked, "Do you believe the power of prayer saved your life?" He replied, "There is not a doubt in my mind that prayer got me through this. God got me through this. These were experienced doctors who looked [my parents] right in the face and said, 'He's not going to make it.'"[3]

When I hear things like this, I imagine two worlds. First there is the natural world. Doctors see and understand this world, and in it, Kirby had no hope. But prayers lifted to God enter the realm of the supernatural, a higher world that will forever elude our best scientific knowledge. God hears the prayers, reaches down into the natural world, and heals Kirby. That seems to be the overall scheme, and I suspect something like it exists in many peoples' minds.

Our Unbiblical Worldview

Miracles occur throughout the Bible. In the Old Testament, earthquakes rumble, locusts swarm, rivers turn to blood, rainbows grace the sky, floods cover the Earth, hungry lions do not eat, rods become snakes, great ghostly hands write on walls, donkeys talk, storms churn the sea, bread falls from heaven, and on and on, all at God's hand. In the Gospels, new stars shine, virgins give birth, and people are raised from the dead, levitate, and are healed of blindness, leprosy, lameness, demon possession, and other grave ills. In the book of Acts, more healings take place, more earthquakes rumble, prison doors are opened, viper bites are rendered ineffective, people suddenly fall dead, and so forth.

The authors of Scripture clearly viewed these events as miraculous. But were the events *equally* miraculous? No. On one hand, you have rainbows and storms at sea, which happen all the time. Today we explain these in purely natural terms. We have no need to bring the supernatural into it at all, so we label these events *non-miraculous*. On the other hand, you have the virgin birth and people being raised from the dead, which do not happen all the time. Science does not apply here. Today we explain these events in purely supernatural terms. We label these events *miraculous*. Finally, you have all the others: healings, new stars, locusts, strangely timed earthquakes, lions that refuse to eat, and so on. These events fall somewhere between the extremes of natural and supernatural. Today we might explain some as purely natural (maybe the star of Bethlehem can be explained by a planetary conjunction, a supernova, or a comet), and some we might describe as purely supernatural (levitation just doesn't happen). But we feel the need to place each event in one of two boxes: natural (not a miracle) or supernatural (a miracle).[4]

The biblical authors felt no such need, because for them, the division between natural and supernatural did not exist. Miracles were special events, but they were easily integrated into a world in which God acted everywhere, sometimes in small ways, sometimes in big ways, but all the time and with human beings in mind. There were miracles and there were nonmiracles, but no bright line was drawn between them. Miracles are woven seamlessly into the Bible's cosmic tapestry.

Our worldview is unbiblical. This is a fact, not a judgment. We see things differently than the authors of Scripture did. The world has changed in many ways since the Bible was written. In particular, science has radically altered our view of God's creation and our place within it. So much can be explained naturally these days. The gulf between the natural and the supernatural spans a great distance, and only God can cross it.

But maybe God can't. A number of prominent scientists claim that science disproves miracles. For them, science has triumphed completely, and no room remains for parting seas, virgin births, wine from water, or resurrection from the dead. Science cannot justify such events, so they must not occur. "Religion believes in miracles, but these aren't compatible with science," said the late, great astrophysicist Stephen Hawking.[5] In his view, reality can be fully explained by natural causes.

Some Christians believe this in their own way or suspect it on some level. After all, miracles do seem scarce these days, suffering is widespread and arbitrary, stories like Grayson Kirby's are rare compared with those having sad endings, and science explains so much. In my experience

Christians are as likely as any other group to be suspicious of miracles.

Anxious Isaac Divides the World

This may be Isaac Newton's fault. He had intense social anxiety and was terrified of the slightest criticism. If you had invited him to your dinner party, he would have spent the evening hiding in a closet, silently judging everyone and thinking about rates of change. But he possessed one of history's truly staggering scientific minds. He is best known for his laws of mechanics and theory of gravity, spelled out in his 1687 work, *Principia.*

His overall view was that objects move because external forces make them move.[6] The word I wish to emphasize is *external*: a thing moves because something outside of it makes it move. The thing itself has no say in the matter. Newton rules out freedom: it moves in exactly this way because of an external force; it moves in exactly that way because of another external force. Causes lead to effects, which themselves are causes for subsequent effects, and so on forever.

For example, a hockey puck moves because it has been slapped by a stick—that is, pushed by a force external to the puck itself. It comes to rest because of friction with the ice, also a force external to the puck itself. It is all mathematically determined.

Now imagine this mechanical viewpoint spreading out to permeate all things and all events, including biological and cultural and artistic and religious activities. There are no surprises in such a universe, and no miracles. If we could somehow know the precise location and speed of every particle in Newton's cosmos at the present time—and in that cosmos, there's no reason in principle why we couldn't—then we could also know the past and predict all events out into the infinite future. This impersonal and closed universe, fixed and predetermined, holds little in common with the God-saturated, miracle-rich world of Scripture.

Newton did not eliminate God or miracles. He believed, as so many of us do, that God stands outside the machinery of the world and reaches in, intervening occasionally to keep things from breaking down. For example, Newton's theory suggested the solar system should fly apart, but it obviously holds together just fine. So he believed its stability (and therefore our survival) was due to God's regular and direct maintenance of planetary orbits.[7] This fits the modern idea of a miracle as a surprising and welcome event that supersedes natural laws and is therefore considered the work of a divine agency. Newton, as much as anyone, separated the natural from the supernatural and laid the foundation for our definition of miracles.

Open and New

Science has moved on since Newton. Aside from evolution and revolutions in geology and astronomy, quantum mechanics was born in the early twentieth century and has matured into a pillar of modern science. It describes truly tiny things—molecules, atoms, atomic nuclei, and individual particles. All things are composed of such tiny objects, of course, so quantum mechanics surrounds us, *is* us.

Quantum mechanics contradicts Newton. The great Englishman cannot guide us down its strange halls. At the quantum level, well-defined and absolute limits restrict what we can know; the future can't be predicted, and the past can't be known, even with perfect knowledge of the present, which we absolutely can't have. Newtonian cause and effect does not exist; matter smooths out into waves, indefinite and ghostlike; systems occupy multiple states at the same time; particles spontaneously pop into and out of existence; and information seems to travel instantaneously from one place to another, apparently breaking even Einstein's cosmic speed limit.[8] This counterintuitive but real world lies at the roots of *everything*.

Quantum mechanics breaks us out of Newton's cause-and-effect straitjacket. This doesn't mean Newton's laws fail to describe the flight of a baseball, or that we need to design buildings with quantum mechanics in mind, or that gravity is a hoax. We do not need to teach Schrödinger's equation, a cornerstone of quantum theory, to engineers who design bridges. Newtonian physics isn't *wrong*; it's just *limited*. Schrödinger's equation contains Newton's laws and may be more amenable to what we call miracles. It doesn't prove miracles, but it allows us to toss out, once and for all, the old, restricting belief that the world is fixed and determined and holds no room for surprises.

But we still rely on our Newtonian reflexes when it comes to miracles. We still assume that we know all the laws of physics there are to know. We still operate as if the laws of physics describe everything there is to describe. We still act as if the phrase *the laws of physics* is more than a metaphor, a way of talking about things. We still believe in two worlds.

Quantum mechanics points out the insufficiency of these ways of thinking. In addition, we have no idea what theory may lurk beneath quantum mechanics.[9] But we *do* know that the world has not been sealed off as a kind of closed mechanism; it unfolds moment by moment, open and always new. The problem is not that matter is all there is but that we think we know what matter is, and we probably don't, even after four hundred years of progress in physics.

"I do not know what I may appear to the world, but to myself I seem to have been only like a boy playing on the sea-shore, and diverting myself in now and then finding a smoother pebble or a prettier shell than ordinary, whilst the great ocean of truth lay all undiscovered before me," said Newton shortly before his death.[10]

The brightest of us stand in a similar relation to the universe and to God.

Back to Max

Before he met Max, Inigo thought there was only *all alive* or *all dead*, one or the other, as if life were operated by a switch. He also thinks Max can flip that switch from off to on. But Max has a larger view: life is operated not by a switch but by a dimmer. A range of possibilities exists between all alive and all dead. Max also knows that the all dead stay all dead. Not even he can bring back someone whose light has gone out completely.

Max's larger view concerns not just life and death but the nature of miracles themselves. From his point of view, no miracles ever occur, at least not the way Inigo thinks of them. Max knows that some things are impossible. But he also knows that many things are possible—things Inigo thinks impossible—and he understands how to do them. Max knows rules and laws and remedies far beyond Inigo's knowledge. From Max's point of view, there are no miracles, just things common people know and things they don't.

Similarly, from God's point of view, there are no miracles, at least not in the way we think of them. Maybe some things are really impossible, even for God. But many things may be possible, even things we think are impossible. Maybe the world works according to laws lying as far beyond our knowledge as quantum mechanics lies beyond the understanding of the average housecat.

It is sometimes stated that the ancients had no way to explain rainbows or earthquakes or healings, so they used God as an explanation. And perhaps people *were* quicker to explain things they didn't understand in terms of the supernatural. Certainly science has allowed us to stop talking about every volcano and earthquake in theological terms. We have learned a lot. But maybe our gullibility simply runs in the opposite direction. If past generations too quickly saw the hand of God in all things, perhaps we too quickly see blind, impersonal forces in all things.

We ourselves have invented the division between the natural and supernatural. It does not correspond to anything in reality. As science fiction pioneer Robert Heinlein put it, *supernatural* is a null word. But if this is true, then *natural* must also be a null word. There is only one world, and God is always working in it. Sometimes this looks like science, and sometimes it looks like a miracle, but it is always there, ever drawing us toward new understandings, new relationships, and new life.

Just ask Miracle Max and the Man in Black.

11.

How to Manufacture a War: History, like the Universe, Is Larger and More Interesting Than You Thought

Galileo Galilei died in 1642, but his body was not placed in its current location, the Basilica of Santa Croce in Florence, until 1737. At that time, someone removed a few fingers and a tooth from the casket. One of those fingers—the middle one from his right hand—has been on display in a Florence museum for years. Withered and brown, the creepy relic seems a little out of place in an exhibit otherwise dedicated to the great scientist's telescopes, inclined planes, and notebooks.

Some years ago, I taught a class on the history of astronomy. Two weeks of lectures and labs were capped by a tour of relevant European cities. We traveled to Krakow, Prague, and Padua and ended our trip in Florence. We visited Museo Galileo, the museum with the finger, on our next-to-last day of the tour.

Up on the third floor, we stood and stared at the weird appendage. After a few minutes, David, one of my students, walked away from the glass case, looked out a window, and began scanning the view. His head craned back and forth.

"What are you doing?" someone asked.

"Trying to get a sense of direction."

"Why?"

"I'm betting the finger's turned toward the Vatican," he said, and everyone laughed out loud.

Two Books You Might Not Want to Take Very Seriously

It would be in fine keeping with history for Galileo's middle finger to be permanently raised toward the seat of the Roman Catholic Church. It was the church, after all, that pressured the great man to deny the truth. Establishing this truth—that Earth moves around the sun and not the other way around—was the work of Galileo's long life, and his forced disavowal humiliated and angered him.

"On his knees, with his hand on the Bible, [Galileo] was compelled to abjure and curse the doctrine of the movement of the earth. What a spectacle! This venerable man, the most illustrious of his age, forced by the threat of death to deny facts which his judges as well as himself knew to be true! He was then committed to prison and treated with remorseless severity during the remaining ten years of his life," writes John William Draper in his 1874 book *History of the Conflict between Religion and Science*.[1] In it he surveys Western history and concludes that, at every turn, the church has gone to war against the growth of scientific knowledge. "The history of Science . . . is a narrative of the conflict of two contending powers, the expansive force of the human intellect on one side, and the compression arising from traditional faith . . . on the other," he writes,[2] and he turns to the Galileo affair as clear proof of his thesis.

Historian Andrew Dickson White presented his own work on the topic in 1896. *A History of the Warfare of Science with Theology in Christendom* provides more detail than Draper's book, but White too casts history in terms of conflict and laments the treatment of Galileo at the hands of the church. "On this champion, Galileo, the whole war was concentrated," White writes. "His discoveries had clearly taken the Copernican theory out of the list of hypotheses, and had placed it before the world as a truth. Against him, the war was long and bitter."[3]

Draper's and White's books were the first to say explicitly that science and faith stand naturally opposed to one another. Both describe science as virtuous and pure, and both present the church as a monolithic force of anti-intellectualism bent on extinguishing the light of progress. Draper's book was read by many, but White's book—long, serious, detailed, and heavily footnoted—looked like real scholarship and had a huge influence. "No work—not even Draper's—has done more than White's to instill in the public mind a sense of the adversarial relationship between science and religion," say historians of science David Lindberg and Ronald Numbers.[4]

But no historian takes these books seriously today; their war talk has been discounted, their claims weakened by lack of evidence. "Refuting [White] is like shooting fish in a barrel. With his combination of bad sources, argument by assertion, quoting out of context, collectivism, and general reliance on exclamation, rather than evidence and argument, White's is not a book to be taken seriously. Its real value is as a relic of its particular time and place, and as a museum of how not to write history," says historian Lawrence Principe in his Great Courses lecture.[5] His assessment is shared by the great majority of contemporary historians.

Reality always turns out to be larger and more interesting than we suspect. The simple notion that science and religion are locked in eternal conflict does not hold up in the face of the evidence, and this begins with Galileo.

Fools, Luminaries, and a Genius

In Padua, my students and I walked through the gilded hall in which Galileo taught. We strolled across the courtyard where he visited with fellow faculty members, and we saw the house where he first turned his telescope to the sky. He discovered the phases of Venus and the "ears" of Saturn (later determined to be rings), and though he never once observed Uranus, he did detect Neptune and noted its apparent motion more than two hundred years before that planet's formal discovery. His early observations of the moon's mountains, the stars of the Milky Way, and four of Jupiter's moons catapulted him to continental fame in 1610.

Well, that and his personality, his rhetorical skills, his knack for marketing, and his political tone-deafness. These factors had as much to do with his stardom as his scientific aptitude. In Galileo we find a singular mix of meticulous observer, crystal-clear scientific thinker, whip-smart debater, salesman, and self-promoter.

His marketing genius is reflected in the fact that his first book—*The Starry Messenger,* in which his early observations were revealed—was published in Italian. The tradition of the day dictated that works of science and philosophy be published in Latin, the language of the learned. Opting for Italian meant that the book could be read by everyone. Galileo knew that lunar mountains, new stars, and moons of Jupiter, though crazy ideas at the time, were simple enough to be grasped by the common person.

Galileo not only did science, he popularized it, and the science he popularized did not sit well with tradition.

Later he began to speak out in favor of a sun-centered universe. This concept did more than push up against tradition; it openly challenged it. University professors, followers of Aristotle and his ancient Earth-centered model, were scandalized. They tried to argue with him, but Galileo could not be outmaneuvered. With barbed wit and spectacular flourish, he soundly demolished his opponents' arguments, humiliating one after another in a series of heavily attended public debates. This was a sure way to entertain audiences and a quick way to make enemies.

The church, which overlapped quite a lot with the universities, eventually got involved. In 1614 in Florence, a friar named Caccini preached a sermon against Galileo. Caccini was scolded for this by his superiors, but a few months later, another churchman penned a letter to the Inquisition, which, thanks to the Protestant Reformation, was operating at maximum force. The letter suggested that Galileo's views might be heretical. But the Inquisition filed the letter away and did not put him on trial or condemn him.

In 1624, Galileo was assured by a supportive Pope Urban VIII that he could discuss the Copernican system, but only as a mathematical theory and not as a physical reality. Galileo was free to treat the sun-centered system as a working hypothesis, but as it had not been proven, he could not teach it as fact.[6]

He was thus released to throw himself into a book on the subject. Known today as the *Dialogue*, it presents a conversation between three fictional characters: Salviati, who argues for the Copernican model; Simplicio, a dull-witted traditionalist who favors the old Earth-centered system; and Sagredo, an intelligent and neutral moderator.

Permission was granted for the book to be published so long as the pope's (and thus the church's) own view was well represented.

But Galileo could not resist the opportunity to score points for himself. Although the *Dialogue* was intended to be a fair and balanced presentation, even a casual reader could see that the Copernican system comes out looking very good while the traditional system does not. Much worse, Galileo made the grave error of putting the pope's very words on the subject into the mouth of the witless Simplicio.

This turned many of his defenders against him and enraged the pope, who brought the Inquisition down on Galileo in 1633. In the end, the great scientist was declared "vehemently suspect of heresy," forced to disavow his beliefs, and sentenced to house arrest. Galileo lived out the remainder of his life at his villa in Arcetri, near Florence, working on a hugely influential treatise on physics, entertaining distinguished visitors, and tending his vineyards. He was not, as Draper put it, "committed to prison and treated with remorseless severity during the remaining ten years of his life."[7]

The War Comes to America

This short and quick version of the Galileo affair reveals no true heroes and no true villains. We could look at it much more carefully, and many historians have done just that. In every case, they've found that the closer you look, the less this chapter of history conforms to the straightforward science-versus-religion myth. Galileo's temperament; the personal affairs of his sympathizers, enemies, and students; the many scientific, theological, and philosophical issues at play; the delicate and multileveled power games played by Rome and Florence; and large-scale European politics mix together to make the Galileo affair impossible to simplify.

That said, it's easy to see how, if Draper and White were looking for a hero, they found one in Galileo. Without question, he stands as a singular genius among a cast ranging from outright fools to mere luminaries. We will never have another like him.

We remember Galileo today because he was right, and on two counts. First, he nailed the narrow question of what goes around what.[8] But he was also right about science itself. At stake in the Galileo affair was not just the arrangement of the planets or even what was true and false. It was concerned with *how we know* what's true and false and *who gets to say* what's true and false. Therefore, the fight had to do with authority and power, and it grew intensely political. If the church had not wielded so much political power, the war might have never arisen in the first place.

But arise it did, and thanks in good part to Draper and White, it came to America. In the early twentieth century, an influential group of Christians began to push back against liberal movements in biblical studies—in particular, an approach to Scripture known as *historical criticism*, which questioned belief in the Bible as a literal document. This group responded to historical criticism by publishing a series of pamphlets entitled *The Fundamentals: A Testimony to the Truth*. The series purported to establish the nonnegotiable truths of Christianity and shored up belief in the factual truth of Genesis, among other things. This conservative resurgence eventually led to the founding of institutions like Biola and Liberty Universities. These fundamentalists (as they came to be known) looked to Draper's and White's books as confirmation that religion and science were naturally opposed to one another.

Wall-to-wall media coverage of the Scopes trial of 1925 brought the war between religion and science to a national audience. Creationism and creation science soon followed. And after 9/11 brought the specter of religious violence to TVs and computer screens worldwide, the New Atheists, next up, bloomed from the well-tended soil of conflict.

12.

Scary Mom and the Atheists: How an Enlarged Faith Reveals the Limits of Science

The lights had been out for about ten minutes when Dan spoke up.

"Paul. Mom's up there. She's doing it again."

"No, she's not. Go to sleep."

Thirty seconds of silence.

"No, I'm serious."

"I am, too. You woke me up. Good night."

More silence.

"I'm telling y—"

"*Whatever*. Look. I'll show you."

I climbed out of bed and felt my way through the dark, heading for the light switch near the bottom of the stairs. My feet made soundless steps on the orange shag carpet in the basement room where Dan, my older brother, and I lived most of our pre-college years.

Some time before this, an event had occurred that I estimate took three to six months off of my life. Mom had tucked Dan and me into bed, said goodnight, ascended the stairs, turned off the light, opened the door, and closed it. She stayed in the room. We couldn't see the top of the stairs, so we had no idea she was up there. After waiting a few minutes for us to settle into happy half-sleep, she crept back down the soft shag stairs in the dark. She got on all fours and crawled quietly to the foot of my bed (the closest one, too bad for me). She found the opening and gently slipped her hand up between the mattress and the sheet. I imagine her pausing briefly again and stifling her laugh before grabbing my nine-year-old ankle and screaming, "*GAAAAA-AAAHHH!*" at the top of her voice.

Now Dan had spoken up, hoping to avoid a replay of this nightmare. I groped and padded my way across the room with the goal of turning on the light and proving him wrong.

But he wasn't wrong. She was waiting under the air hockey table this time. The table stood between my bed and the light switch at the bottom of the stairs. She launched herself at me, hands first, as I passed.

"*GRRAAAA-AAhhh aahaahhhh, got you! Haaaaaha HAHA hahahh! Oh, hahahaHA!*" To this day, Mom cries whenever her laughter becomes uncontrollable, and she was really crying that night.

Late one winter afternoon, when Dan and I were in high school, she moved her car out of our carport and parked it around the corner. Then she walked back to the house, locked herself in, turned off all the lights, and waited for us to get home. We pulled into the driveway of the dark, seemingly empty house and let ourselves in. By this time, she had hidden in the hall closet, prepared for the ultimate jump scare and another fit of joyful, riotous laughter. She got both, because she had thought it out so well. It's the careful preparation that really impresses.

Over time, I grew nervous every time I heard an unusual noise, came home to find the house unexpectedly empty, or spent time at home alone at night. Scary Mom altered the quality of my life so that nearly every unusual occurrence at home prompted mild anxiety. Over time, being scared of being scared became more crippling than simply being scared.

Only Mom's closest family and friends know of her appetite for terrifying innocent people. You'd never guess it, meeting her. She is one of those gregarious Southern women who make new friends everywhere they go. She has decades-long relationships with local shop owners. She chats up children in the checkout line. She makes brownies for her roof guys. But she also scares the life out of those closest to her, over and over and over, and she thinks it's *hilarious.*

We suspect this quirk of her personality originates from her own childhood. Her older brother terrorized her regularly and gleefully, especially when their parents were out of the house. Whatever its source, the truth remains: I spent much of my youth scared of being scared by my own mother.

The Four Horsemen Pay a Visit to My Soul

Being raised this way has had its effects on me. Besides having a shortened life span, I too find it amusing when people get suddenly scared without danger. Also, Halloween has become my favorite holiday. The emotional, religious, and social pressures of most holidays tend to shut me down. But in October, there's less stress, and I happily celebrate the annual cooling of Atlanta by laughing at what scares me.

Every Halloween, I write down my fears, and one by one, I laugh at them. I laugh at cancer, at the vulnerability of my children, at financial concerns, at my regrets, at the future, at my shortcomings. These things can overwhelm me on any given day, but once a year, I set them in their proper place. Laughter has a way with fear. Like love, laughter drives it out.

I also make a list of things that used to scare me. Scary Mom is on this list, as is quicksand, lava, *The Shining*, and the New Atheists, a group led by the so-called Four Horsemen of Richard Dawkins, Sam Harris, Daniel Dennett, and the late Christopher Hitchens. A few years back, they all wrote books about how reason and science demonstrate the childishness and irrationality and harmfulness of religion. Their arguments were not new, but their target was. They rejected—and still reject—all religious belief of all faiths and all kinds, without exception, no matter how crass or sophisticated. Their disdain runs from the grossest fundamentalism to the most rarefied academic theology. All of it, they say, should go.

It began with the publication of Harris's *The End of Faith* in 2005. I was instantly and morbidly fascinated. For years, I read the Horsemen's books, lurked about their blogs, and came to know a number of atheists personally. My fascination persisted long enough to baffle me: Why should I care so much?

It was a scary question. As a professor of physics and astronomy, I told myself that I care because the New Atheists say science (of all things) disproves the claims of faith. During my seminary years, I told myself that I cared out of theological interest. But what really frightened me was the possibility that the New Atheists were right.

The Other Side of Faith

By the time the Four Horsemen showed up, I had already seriously doubted my faith at least three times. The first time happened when I was a child. My parents split up when I was five, and I began to suspect that God was not there. (Scary Mom is my stepmom, but we call her Mom.) This fear brought nightmares and deep sadness and a conviction that things in this world cannot be counted on to work properly.

The second wave of doubt, described in the early chapters of this book, arrived when I was a young man. This was not scary. Christianity just seemed so unlikely. Looking back, I can see that this episode was really a matter of me shedding a particular set of childhood beliefs, beliefs that looked pretty naive and irrational next to science.

The third time occurred shortly after I came back to the Christian faith. One of my friends gave me a book. It was written before the rise of the New Atheists but argued like them that science disproves God. By the third chapter, I grew so scared that I put it down and didn't pick it back up for years. It was the same old childhood fear, brought to me this time at the hands of science.

The New Atheists scared me, too. I began to wonder if these horsemen were right and, unlike me, had the conviction to speak out. Perhaps my fascination resulted from my own unconscious unbelief. I began to ask myself, "Do I need to just grow up and face the truth? Does a larger freedom await on the other side of faith? Am I a closet atheist?" The thought terrified me, but today I view the New Atheists with the kind of bemused curiosity reserved for things that used to scare me but don't anymore, like lava and Scary Mom.

I'm not afraid, and for two reasons. First, I tried on atheism, but it didn't fit. I couldn't pull it off. I opened myself up to the very real possibility that I didn't believe in God, but I never felt the click of discovery. It never felt true. My belief in God has so merged with my deepest identity that

I simply can't cast it aside. Stop believing in God? I might as well stop believing in my own existence.

Second, my faith has shown me the limits of science, which reveals how the universe works; tells us deep truths about the nature of energy and matter and our material origins; and helps us build better can openers and grow taller basketball players. But science cannot reveal all things, and it refuses to acknowledge whole classes of questions that are important to everyone—questions concerning good and evil, purpose, and meaning.

Jesus and Mohammed Walk into a Bar

Jesus and Mo is a satirical online comic strip in which Jesus and the prophet Mohammed talk to one another and to an invisible (and skeptical) barmaid. It means to mock religion, but one particular strip illustrates my point about science. Jesus and Mohammed are at the bar as usual, this time talking science and religion.

Jesus speaks first: "Science is fine as far as it goes, but it cannot answer the big questions such as 'Why are we here?' And 'What is the purpose of beauty?'"

Mohammed agrees and adds another: "Who created the laws of physics and logic?"

Jesus declares for both of them: "These are questions for *theologians* to answer."

The barmaid says, "Do theologians really have answers to these questions? I thought they just made answers up."

To which Jesus says, "Exactly! Science is limited by its refusal to *make stuff up*."

"This is what gives religion its *edge*," asserts an agreeable Mohammed, wrapping up the four-panel strip.[1]

Jesus is right: science is limited by its refusal to make stuff up, if by "make stuff up" he means taking seriously anything that's not grounded in the methods and theories of science. If this is what Jesus means, then we all make stuff up every day. We *have to,* because no one lives their lives in strict accordance to the truths and methods of science alone. And everybody lives according to virtues like love that have nothing to do with empirical science.

Science can shape the way you think. It can prevent you from believing nonsense. It provides an infinite supply of wonder. But science alone will not help you navigate the challenges and heartbreaks and joys that are part of every human life. In this sense, science is hollow. It will not give us morally satisfying answers to Jesus's questions: "Why are we here?" and "What is the purpose of beauty?" It can't console a mother who has lost a child. It can't tell us how we are to live. It can't fill our everyday lives with meaning and direction. Science alone will not tell us how to respond to injustice or oppression or violence.

Creatures of Love

Consider this unavoidable question: What is a human being? If we ask science this question, it replies that a human being is a creature genetically related to all others, an organism within an environment. It is a complicated organism, yes, and its environment has cultural as well as biological components, but no qualitative distinction can be made between *Homo sapiens* and other animals. We may be unique, but blobfish and silverback gorillas and Venus flytraps are unique, too.

On a more basic level, science says a human being is a collection of about a million billion trillion atoms (that's 1,000,000,000,000,000,000,000,000,000,000). About 62 percent of these atoms are hydrogen, 24 percent are oxygen, 12 percent are carbon, and 1 percent are nitrogen; traces of calcium, phosphorus, potassium, sulfur, and about fifty other elements also are found in the human body. Science also tells us that these atoms must be arranged in a very particular and complex way, and thanks to billions of years of evolution, they have been. The atoms themselves are neither living nor conscious, but when they are arranged in this way, both life and consciousness somehow emerge from them. This is weird and wonderful.

But it's limited. To see this, let's ask Christianity the same question: What is a human being? Like science, it says we are creatures, organisms within an environment. It not only acknowledges but embraces the wonder and mystery of our physical bodies of atoms and molecules and cells and evolution and consciousness. Christianity contains all of this. It recognizes and celebrates our physicality. Faith has no argument with scientific accounts of *Homo sapiens.*

But it goes further. It takes what science says, interprets it, and "makes stuff up," in the words of cartoon Jesus. Its data set includes and surpasses the biological and physical to encompass the emotional, social, and spiritual. Faith takes into account not only the objective features of human bodies and the universe but also the subjective experiences and meanings of millions of individual and communal lives.

So when it comes to human beings, faith says we are organisms-plus. It says we are organisms that *bear the image of God* (Genesis 1:27). Lots of ideas have been proposed about the meaning of this phrase. Some say it means we have some skill or capacity that sets us apart from other animals. This might be reason or creativity or the use of language, but whatever it is makes us kind of like God. Others say the image of God is relational. This means we relate more intimately with God and with each other than other creatures do. Still others say that we are like God because we have dominion over the Earth and other creatures just as God has dominion over all creation.

However you think about the image of God, it's clear that *love* has something to do with it. Scripture and Christian tradition say we were created out of love and for love. God, in whom we live and move and have our being, *is* love (Acts 17:28; 1 John 4:8). The Gospel of Mark tells the story of a scribe who asks Jesus, "What is the greatest commandment?" Jesus replies, "The first is, 'Hear, O Israel: the Lord our God, the Lord is one; you shall love the Lord your God with all your heart, and with all your soul, and with all your mind, and with all your strength.' The second is this, 'You shall love your neighbor as yourself.' There is no other commandment greater than these" (12:29–31). Love is why we are here, and love is how we should live.

So we are creatures of love, and love and fear cannot coexist. "There is no fear in love, but perfect love casts out fear" (1 John 4:18a). And Jesus, whom the writer of Colossians calls *the* image of God (1:15), fully embodies this love and lack of fear. That's why he is so important.

You won't learn about any of this from science. The divine image is not a scientifically verifiable idea. Neither is love. Science also cannot *contradict* these things. They simply exist in the land beyond science.

If everything beyond the borders of science is made up, then the question is not whether we should make stuff up; it is *what kind* of stuff we should make up. As followers of Jesus, we reach for love, a very fine made-up thing indeed.

And our faith is nothing less than a love story big enough to contain science and the cosmos it reveals, open enough to take all questions, and generous enough to set all human creatures free to laugh at everything that scares them.

13.

Why I Came Back: Love Embraces the Cosmos

My childhood faith was gone by the time I left home for college, and there I found little to draw me back. My professors were secular. I made friends of different faith backgrounds and of no faith background. As a freshman, I roomed with a practicing Hindu. As a sophomore, I took a course in Eastern religions that radically expanded my perspective.

But none of this made Christianity unattractive. That job was accomplished by the students in the Christian organizations. They were no less prone to backbiting and foolishness than anyone else, but their claims about being "not perfect, just forgiven" made them look especially ridiculous.

I adopted the point of view that the whole Christian thing was probably not true, and I let it go. It was painless. I declared a major in physics. My science courses increased my knowledge and love of the cosmos and made my boyhood faith look even smaller and more irrelevant by comparison.

My appearance changed along with my thinking. I grew my hair out past my shoulders and took to wearing old army jackets and decaying black Chuck Taylors. I rarely shaved. I played in extremely loud rock bands and hung out with guys who smoked a lot of dope. We spent our week-ends sitting around in clouds of yellow smoke, listening to Frank Zappa and playing parties and bars.

I transferred to a new college between my sophomore and junior years. I lived off campus and didn't know many people, so I spent my afternoons studying in the student center. My ready availability and shabby appearance attracted the Baptist students, who tried to convert me.

I recall one conversation in particular. I was sitting by myself when Matthew walked up. He was a friendly fellow who reminded me of B. J. Hunnicutt from the *M*A*S*H* reruns I watched as a teenager.

"Hi, Paul. May I sit down?" he asked.

"Sure. Have a seat," I said.

I knew what he was up to. He was known for helping people like me. Starting it myself wasn't an option, so I made small talk until he began.

"Let me ask you a question," he said.

"Okay."

"What do you think is the bigger sin: stealing a pen or murdering a child?" This was a new angle. It took me by surprise.

"Uh, the murder?"

"No, that's not right. It says in the Bible that all sins are equally reprehensible before God."

"That's crazy. I don't believe that."

"Yeah, it's in the book of—"

"That's not what I mean," I countered. "Please don't start with the Bible. Start with the actual three-dimensional world. The consequences of the murder are huge. Think of the parents' pain. They would be scarred for life, and siblings, too. No one cares if you steal their pen."

"God does."

"Maybe. But not as much as he cares about a child's life and a family's happiness."

"Any stain on you is unbearable to God," he said.

"Well, too bad for me."

"No, that's where Jesus comes in . . . "

I don't remember how it ended, but I definitely won the argument. Winning arguments was super easy, I discovered, so long as I was the judge. I loved this kind of thing. Others came at me also, and I would challenge them with evolution and with the problem of evil, the inconsistencies of Scripture, or whatever was on my mind that day. It was fun, and there were benefits: so long as Christians saw me as a conversion project and not as a fellow human being trying to figure it out like everyone else, I could keep my distance from them, and I could do it with integrity.

My arguments worked as well as arguments can, I suppose, but now I know that my opposition to these Christians was not grounded in reason but in identity. My real problem was that they dressed the way Mom always wanted me to dress—everything neat and clean and tucked in. You got the idea that their theology had the same characteristics, and I was not interested in that kind of thinking.

This went on until September of my senior year. That's when I met Elizabeth, a Christian I couldn't argue with. I don't mean she had all the answers or was a skilled debater. She just didn't argue. She had no interest in it. And it didn't matter how she dressed or what her theology was, because on the day I met her, sitting in the same room where I had spoken with Matthew a year earlier, she looked at me and didn't see a conversion project or a physics major or a freaky rock musician. I felt like she saw *me* beneath all that, and she had no agenda. This immediately shut down the rather prominent smart-ass component of my persona, which was unpleasant.

It would've been easy to be her project. I could've written her off and gotten on with my life. But we got along *so well*. We talked for hours, night after night, with zero effort. It was the first time I had ever dated someone and not gotten all locked up by nerves and self-consciousness. But the faith thing held us back. She had it and I didn't, and that mattered to both of us.

Over the next six months, she stood still as I skittered toward her and away from her like a nervous squirrel. It caused her some pain, but she held out. In the level gaze of her love, I eventually calmed down, began to pray with her, and months later, attended church with her. Within two years of meeting, we were joined in Christian marriage.

And Now, a Word about Lobsters

To grow, a lobster must periodically molt, or shed its skin. Molting occurs when a lobster's shell becomes so tight and cramped that the creature can no longer do normal lobster things. So the hard shell cracks, and the lobster pushes backward out of it. It's a stressful but necessary process. A newly molted lobster is vulnerable to injury and disease because its new shell is very soft, so it hides for several weeks while its fresh skin hardens into a new, larger shell. A lobster molts more than a dozen times on its way to adulthood. If it did not molt, it would die.

Along my faith journey, I have molted many times. I have shed old, cramped beliefs in exchange for newer, roomier ones. As a high schooler, I thought I was losing my faith, and during college, I figured I had lost it for good. But I had only shed certain childhood concepts about God, myself, and the world—that God was basically like my dad, only larger and invisible; that my particular religious upbringing provided the one true perspective; that the cosmos was made especially for human beings. Over time, these ideas became restrictive and grew hard, cracked, and fell away. Science emerged to take their place.

This new shell worked for a while, but like all shells, it didn't last. Like my childhood faith before it, science alone proved too limiting. I needed more; I needed science-plus. Elizabeth's invitation to love was a call for me to molt yet again, to leave behind belief in science alone in favor of a larger view.

Three Voices

So it was love, not science or an argument, that brought me back and opened up my world.

Arguments and knowledge and logic help me do science, teach, make personal decisions, plan for the future, write books, raise children, drive a car, vote, and do a thousand other good and necessary things. As it goes for me, so it goes for all of us. When reason and logic break down, the whole world stops working the way it should. More than this, these things carry us forward. They help us discover relativity, cure diseases, explore Mars, and turn dreams into realities.

None of this is opposed to love. Love and reason work together like faith and science. And in the same way that faith must contain all science, love must encompass all reason and knowledge and sound argument. Love puts these tools in their proper context and sets them to their rightful task of building a better and more just and more beautiful world.

Jesus said, "Love the Lord your God with all your heart, and with all your soul, and with all your strength, and with *all your mind*" (Luke 10:27a, italics added).

The apostle Paul said, "If I *understand all mysteries and*

all knowledge, but do not have love, I am nothing." (1 Corinthians 13:2, italics added).

Mister Rogers said, "Love is at the root of everything: *all learning,* all relationships. Love or the lack of it."[1]

These trusted voices assure us that all knowledge and all learning, including science, rest upon the foundation of love. But knowledge, scientific and otherwise, can become separated from love and be used for self-serving ends. Knowledge is power, after all, and science in particular offers us power unlike anything else. It has been used to prop up racism, develop unspeakable weapons of war, invade individual privacy, manipulate elections, and pollute the planet. New Atheists use science to devalue other forms of knowledge. Creationists employ their strange and stunted version of science to misrepresent the truth and manipulate people.

We can also abuse knowledge in small personal situations. Once removed from love, knowledge can act as a kind of security blanket, protecting us from our anxiety about not knowing. It can be used to push others away. I did this with Matthew. My discussion with him was not grounded in love, and I had as little interest in knowing him as he did in knowing me. I did not have a relationship with him, I had a strategy: the calculated deployment of knowledge. I just wanted to win. But Elizabeth opted for love, and that made all the difference.

Love and Quasars

Today I know that science separated from faith, like knowledge separated from love, is no more than a noisy gong and clanging cymbal. I also know why Dad told everyone that story about my seeing the glory of God in a set of Arkansas sunbeams.

He didn't do it to make me seem simple. He didn't do it to mock me. He told the story because it was a true moment. There in the car, looking out across the rice fields, I saw something beautiful, and I responded without calculation: *That is the glory of God.* The words were plain and un-self-conscious. My heart and mind and speech were unified in that moment, and Dad saw me clearly, just as Elizabeth saw me on the day she met me, and it made him love me. Telling that story was his way of connecting with me, of returning to and remembering who I am and who he was. What I hated was that he knew me so well and told everyone about me. I didn't like being found out.

I never understood this until I became a father myself, but there is a sense in which children remain themselves their whole life long. Growing up, I thought there would come a day when I'd stop finding God in creation. I would get to a certain age or take a certain job or learn a certain amount of stuff, and my habit of stopping in my tracks to stare in silence at birds and leaves and stars would end. At some stage, the sunbeams and bugs and night sky would fade, and I would get on with the work of being a functioning, mortgage-holding, taxpaying adult. But this never happened. Oh, I function, I suppose, and I certainly pay taxes, but the God-in-creation thing has only grown stronger, and there's nothing I can do about it.

My professional life made it possible for me to not stop. Though I didn't know it at the time, I became a scientist so I could remain close to God. In my life as a research physicist, I worked in two directions and ended up in two equally remote locations. As a graduate student and postdoctoral associate, I studied atomic nuclei. With our trusty particle accelerator, my colleagues and I drilled down into the heart of matter and mapped out previously unknown details of certain nuclei. We were captained down the rabbit hole by quantum mechanics, that strange but reliable guide to the world of the ultra-tiny.

As an astrophysicist, I traveled in the other direction. As I've mentioned, our group worked on quasars, among the most distant objects ever studied. The light we detected from that one quasar traveled for seven billion years before being intercepted by NASA's orbiting telescope. It had already been traveling for over two billion years when the solar system began to form. It sailed on across the universe as life appeared and evolved, as untold waves of life and death washed across the face of the world, and as certain African hominids stood up, threw their heads back in wonder, became human, and discovered love and quasars.

Operating the proton accelerator, performing high-resolution gamma-ray spectroscopy, sifting through astronomical data, writing code for data analysis, and teaching relativity and quantum mechanics and astrophysics have kept me in proximity to the glory of God revealed to me that November day in eastern Arkansas. I am continually perplexed by those who claim that science is anti-God.

Great and Shining

At some point on my faith journey, I discovered that the more you learn, the more you realize you don't know. Knowledge is like a spotlight on a dark stage: the larger the pool of light, the longer the boundary between it and the surrounding darkness. This boundary, which is awareness of your not-knowing, grows in proportion to the light of understanding. Your ignorance can be known, but like any other thing worth knowing, it must be learned.

Today we know enough to say with confidence that we understand little. We gaze into atomic nuclei and find a strange and alien world of particles moving like ghosts through emptiness unimaginable, a world of questions. We look into our own selves and into the eyes of our neighbor and find there a depth that can only be compared to the universe itself, a universe we have been searching for thousands of years, and still we do not know what we are looking at.

Search the cosmos, and you will find no bottom and no boundaries, but faith can contain it still. God does not explain the world the way gravity or evolution does, and faith does not compete with science. God is not a theory of everything. God does not close the door on our not-knowing but throws it open and invites us to experience the joy of knowing and to deepen the great mystery of not knowing.

God is not knowledge but love, a love embracing all knowing and all not-knowing, a love in which fear—of the unknown, of our own questions, even of death—has no place. And we are perhaps the strangest of all things: walking, talking assemblies of atoms that have found ourselves in an infinite and evolving universe that somehow makes no sense and carries no meaning and offers no hope outside the great and shining reality we call love.

Endnotes

Introduction

1. The earliest verifiable and unambiguous Uranus joke is found in the March 30, 1881, issue of *Puck*, a New York–based satirical magazine. For details, see Albert Stern, "A Deep Dive into Uranus Jokes," Electric Lit, November 17, 2017, https://tinyurl.com/y9lzq2p2.

2. See "Six Reasons Young Christians Leave Church," Barna, 2011, https://tinyurl.com/ya2tfhbd.

Chapter 1: Two Ways of Seeing the Sun: Through the Eyes of Faith or the Eyes of Science?

1. Francis's "Canticle of the Sun" can be found at Catholic Online, tinyurl.com/ycekg9j7.

2. Alice Calaprice, ed., *The Quotable Einstein* (Princeton, NJ: Princeton University Press, 2005), 208.

Chapter 2: I'm Pretty Sure My Life Was Changed by a Second-Grade Field Trip: The Problem Shows Up and Grows Up

1. Other possibilities exist, all of them equally bleak. This theory is the current leader.

2. Yes, Uranus, like the other gas giants, has rings around it.

3. We have limited ourselves to Christian communities. The world of faith far exceeds this limit!

4. These four relationships have been promoted by Ian Barbour in books such as *When Science Meets Religion* (New York: HarperCollins, 2000). He refers to them as *conflict*, *independence*, *dialogue*, and *integration*.

Chapter 3: How Not to Chessbox: Faith and Science Face Off

1. See Ken Ham, "Dinosaurs and the Bible," Answers in Genesis, November 5, 1999, https://tinyurl.com/yc3ng623.

2. Richard Dawkins, *The Blind Watchmaker* (London: W. W. Norton, 1996), 448–49.

3. See Daniel G. Taylor, BibViz, bibviz.com, for a fun interactive version.

4. Sam Harris, *The Moral Landscape* (New York: Free Press, 2010), 2.

5. See Gleb Tsipursky, "Using Science, Not Religion, to Find Your Purpose," Richard Dawkins Foundation for Reason and Science, April 21, 2015, https://tinyurl.com/y9apd9bk.

Chapter 4: Strangers, Friends, Lovers: Cooperation, Not Competition

1. I don't believe that faith and science are best described as strangers, but my answer was appropriate for a middle-schooler thinking about these things for the first time.

2. Stephen Jay Gould, "Nonoverlapping Magisteria," *Natural History* 106 (March 1997): 16–22, available at Unofficial Stephen Jay Gould Archive, https://tinyurl.com/y8bnpkph.

3. See See Nicholas Bakalarfeb, "On Evolution, Biology Teachers Stray From Lesson Plan," *New York Times*, February 7, 2011, https://tinyurl.com/y9poaxuv.

Chapter 5: A Universe with a Point: How Science Enlarges Faith

1. Cosmic gamma rays don't damage living things on Earth's surface (or turn them into large, green, angry monsters) because they are absorbed high in the atmosphere. Detecting them requires the use of orbiting telescopes such as Fermi (see Goddard Space Flight Center, "Celebrating 10 Years of Fermi," NASA, June 11, 2018, https://tinyurl.com/yd9oj3m7) and INTEGRAL (see European Space Agency, "INTEGRAL," https://tinyurl.com/y8peeogs).

2. Steven Weinberg, *The First Three Minutes: A Modern View of the Origin of the Universe* (New York: Basic, 1977), 154.

3. Martin Luther King Jr., "Our God Is Marching On!," March 25, 1965, The Martin Luther King, Jr. Research

and Education Institute, Stanford University, https://tinyurl.com/yyd5ukk8.

4. Other roads exist. For example, Buddhism rejects all such speculation, existentialism accepts the first path but goes on to insist that authentic individuals create their own meaning through their commitments, and Hinduism posits a cyclical cosmos. But this book does not argue that the Christian faith stands as the sole alternative to scientific materialism, only that it is not inconsistent with science.

5. P. Z. Myers, *The Happy Atheist* (New York: Vintage, 2014), 97.

6. Sociobiology, a field of study promoted by biologist and author E. O. Wilson, among others, draws all human social behavior, including religious belief and practice, under the umbrella of science. Wilson travels the first road, viewing religious faith as a trait selected to increase our chances of survival. Others, like the late Stephen Jay Gould, consider faith to be a secondary side effect of evolution, or "spandrel."

Chapter 6: A Larger, Stranger God: How Science Expands Your View of God

1. Like Beyoncé and Kanye, Tycho (pronounced *tee*-kō) goes by his first name.

2. There's *Uran-* again; in Greek mythology, Urania is the muse of astronomy, and Uranus is the god of the sky. Uraniborg translates to "castle of the sky."

3. Tycho didn't live long enough to see Johannes Kepler, one of his research assistants, use his own hard-won naked-eye data to prove Copernicus right.

4. It's easy to be amused by the ignorance of our ancestors, but what evidence do *you* have that Earth moves

around the sun? Almost certainly you have none, other than the word of your fourth-grade teacher and NASA. It's really a subtle argument involving Newton's laws and a phenomenon called the *aberration of starlight*. The fact of Earth's motion belongs in the category Not Obvious.

5. Tycho believed the closest stars were about fifty-two million miles from Earth, but if Copernicus was right, then they had to lie at a distance of *at least* thirty-six billion miles. This was, for him, altogether too much empty space.

6. Victor Thoren, *The Lord of Uraniborg* (New York: Cambridge University Press, 1990), 304.

7. Alpha Centauri's three stars cannot be resolved with the naked eye. Without a telescope, they look like a single bright star.

8. A light-year is the distance light travels in a year, about six trillion miles. Similarly, a light-hour is nearly six hundred million miles, about a third of the distance between the sun and Uranus. Tycho thought the distance between Saturn and the stars was no more than about five light-minutes, or about six-tenths of the actual distance between the sun and Earth.

9. No one knows why. This discovery, made by two independent teams of researchers, led to the proposal of what we call *dark energy*. We don't know what this energy is (hence the name), but we can measure its effect: the acceleration of cosmic expansion.

Chapter 7: Not Even Wrong: How Science Releases the Bible from Literalism

1. Einstein disliked the name *relativity* because it is misleading. The fundamental point of relativity is not that time

and space are relative, which they are, but that the laws of physics are *not* relative.

2. See Gerald Schroeder, *Genesis and the Big Bang* (New York: Bantam, 1990). Schroeder uses *general relativity* to do this, whereas the Anna-and-Bob example employs *special relativity*. The special theory is a subset of the general.

3. "Wolfgang Ernst Pauli, 1900–1958," *Biographical Memoirs of Fellows of the Royal Society* 5 (February 1960): 186, doi.org/10.1098/rsbm.1960.0014.

4. In the early seventeenth century, Archbishop James Ussher, using the Bible only, calculated that creation began at 6:00 p.m. on October 22, 4004 BCE.

5. This is the same method Tycho Brahe used, unsuccessfully, to determine the distances to the stars. Also, our eyes and brain use parallax to produce depth perception for nearby objects.

6. This quote is drawn from Galileo's "Letter to the Grand Duchess Christina of Tuscany," his fullest opinion on the relationship between religion and science. See it at https://tinyurl.com/yyuoo6wc.

Chapter 8: A Scientist Reads the Bible: How Science Enlarges Scripture

1. See "Man Out to Prove the World Is Flat Crashes Homemade Rocket," YouTube, 1:38, uploaded by "Inside Edition," March 26, 2018, tinyurl.com/y74lrms6.

2. See Graham Ambrose, "These Coloradans Say Earth Is Flat, and Gravity's a Hoax; Now, They're Being Persecuted," *Denver Post*, July 7, 2017, https://tinyurl.com/yd2d75z7.

3. Binoculars are not strictly necessary, but they make the job easier.

4. Universal Time (UT) is derived from the mean solar time along the Prime Meridian, which runs through the observatory at Greenwich, London. It is often used when referring to events that occur on a global scale.

5. See National Centers for Environmental Information, "December 26, 2004 Sumatra, Indonesia Earthquake and Tsunami—Tenth Anniversary Update," December 11, 2014, https://tinyurl.com/y4ntlmeg.

6. For example, see Shannon Hall, "Earth's Tectonic Activity May Be Crucial for Life—and Rare in Our Galaxy," *Scientific American*, July 20, 2017, https://tinyurl.com/y9pj3xkl.

Chapter 9: The Things God Has Made: How Science Enlarges Our View of Life and Death

1. It is often claimed that Augustine's answer to the question "What was God doing before he created heaven and earth?" was "Preparing hell for people who asked such questions." This is false.

2. He was right until the early twentieth century, anyway, when Einstein showed up. Now he's just *mostly* right.

3. These events probably last several thousand years. Many scientists believe we are currently in the midst of a human-driven extinction event.

4. Whether or not you believe in the virgin birth, the point remains (the question of the virgin birth and other miracles comes up in the next chapter).

Chapter 10: At Home with Miracle Max: How Science Expands Our Understanding of Miracles

1. All quotes in this section are from *The Princess Bride*, dir. Rob Reiner (1987; 20th Century Fox).

2. Lacey Rollins and Tracy Sears, "Doctors Can't Explain Grayson Kirby's Miraculous Recovery," WTVR, August 11, 2014, https://tinyurl.com/yyygzsyx.

3. "Grayson Kirby Shares Miraculous Survival Story on the Steve Harvey Show," YouTube, 1:09, uploaded by "WTVR CBS 6," October 14, 2014, https://youtu.be/RnJoFO0Trag.

4. This felt need is related to God-of-the-gaps thinking, introduced in chapter 9, which places acts of God into the supernatural, impossible-to-explain-by-science box.

5. See Chris Matyszczyk, "Stephen Hawking Makes It Clear: There Is No God," *CNet*, September 26, 2014, https://tinyurl.com/y7lkdrbu.

6. This is technically incorrect, because only *changes* in the motion of an object are due to external forces, but it will do for our purpose.

7. The stability of the solar system is still a topic of debate more than three hundred years after Newton. For example, see Scott Tremaine, "Is the Solar System Stable?," Institute for Advanced Study, 2011, https://tinyurl.com/yaqxgd4s.

8. We don't think it does, though; see "Questions about

the Theory of Relativity," Ask an Astronomer, n.d., https://tinyurl.com/yd468zmq.

9. String theory is one candidate, but there are many versions of it. We remain far from a solution.

10. David Brewster, *Memoirs of the Life, Writings, and Discoveries of Sir Isaac Newton*, vol. 2 (Edinburgh: T. Constable, 1855), 420, http://tinyurl.com/yyrw8hhr.

Chapter 11: How to Manufacture a War: History, like the Universe, Is Larger and More Interesting Than You Thought

1. John William Draper, *History of the Conflict between Religion and Science* (New York: D. Appleton & Sons, 1875), 171–72, https://tinyurl.com/y5rw3nkj.

2. Draper, *History of the Conflict*, vi, https://tinyurl.com/yyto2kc9.

3. Andrew D. White, *A History of the Warfare of Science with Theology in Christendom* (New York: D. Appleton, 1901), 130, https://tinyurl.com/y3v9wvwn.

4. See David C. Lindberg and Ronald L. Numbers, "Beyond War and Peace: A Reappraisal of the Encounter between Christianity and Science," *Perspectives on Science and Christian Faith* 39, no. 3 (September 1987): 140–49, available at https://tinyurl.com/y8gaqprh.

5. Lawrence M. Principe, "The Warfare Thesis," Lecture 2 in *Science and Religion*, The Great Courses, (DVD, The Teaching Company, 2006). One of White's most telling errors is his insistence that, in order to gain support for his journeys, Christopher Columbus had to fight against the church's belief in a flat Earth.

6. Contrary to White's and Draper's claims and to pop-

ular belief, Galileo never proved that Earth goes around the sun. He disproved Aristotle's theory, but this was not the same as proving his own. At the time, a third theory, developed by Tycho Brahe, was favored by most European astronomers, but Galileo never mentioned it in any of his publications.

7. Draper, *History of the Conflict*, 172, https://tinyurl.com/y5wummc6.

8. But not completely. Galileo held onto a lot of old and wrong astronomical ideas like circular motion and a strange geometric device called the *epicycle*. Both were relegated to the Dustbin of Bad Scientific Ideas shortly after Galileo's death. Johannes Kepler, Galileo's contemporary and first public supporter, rejected these ideas while embracing the sun-centered model. He therefore got closer to the truth of things than Galileo did.

Chapter 12: Scary Mom and the Atheists: How an Enlarged Faith Reveals the Limits of Science

1. Mohammed Jones (pseud.), *Jesus and Mo*, August 17, 2011, https://tinyurl.com/y94bkspw.

Chapter 13: Why I Came Back: Love Embraces the Cosmos

1. *Won't You Be My Neighbor*, official trailer, Focus Features, 2 min. 39 sec., March 20, 2018, available on YouTube at https://tinyurl.com/yd6nobe6 (italics added).